Paperweights
for Collectors

Mt. Washington rose.

Paperweights for Collectors

An illustrated history
and identification guide
for antique and
modern paperweights

Lawrence H. Selman
Linda Pope-Selman

Paperweight Press • Santa Cruz, California

First Edition

This printing is limited to
two-thousand copies
of which this is No. 1429

Copyright © 1975 by Paperweight Press
Post Office Box 400, Santa Cruz, CA 95060
Library of Congress Catalog Card No. 75-37108

Printed and bound in the United States of America
by Taylor Publishing Company, Dallas, Texas.

Dedication

To Paul Jokelson, for his encouragement and tireless efforts toward the advancement of fine art paperweights.

To our mothers, for the tireless efforts and continuing encouragement they have given to us.

Acknowledgements

We would like to thank the many private collectors and the Edward L. Doheny Memorial Library for allowing us to photograph their treasured paperweights. The John Nelson Bergstrom Art Center and Museum kindly supplied photographs from its collection, including figures 151, 157, 185, 195, 197, 198.

We are very appreciative to Perthshire Paperweights and Lundberg Studios for allowing us to photograph their production.

Many thanks to Fred Koger for technical advice and production assistance above and beyond the call of duty.

Additional thanks to Les Pacholski and Vicki Knox for their assistance and Cynthia Mathews for artistic advice, loyal support and general encouragement.

Table of Contents

Preface

As we look back over the years, we're continually impressed at how life's apparently random experiences led us into a completely new and rewarding field. Early in our married life our total assets consisted of a Ph.D. in chemistry, a love of early music and a position with the airlines. Paperweights did not exist for us.

Our introduction to this specialized world came from a friend whose eclectic interests and varied expertise had always astounded us. We visited him often in his remote and rustic home; he always seemed to surprise us with something new, from a collection of fine Japanese prints, to a rich appreciation of American folk traditions. On one visit he brought out his paperweight collection. He spent hours explaining his collection to us, pointing out the intricacies of millefiori canes that give clue to a weight's origin, discussing the different motifs, and giving a vivid account of the history and love associated with collecting.

Also about that time we had begun to poke around antique shops, just snooping for any inexpensive item that took our fancy. When in the course of one afternoon's browsing we came across a dusty, old paperweight with a Clichy signature cane and a $40 price tag, we simply couldn't believe it.

We came to learn what early collectors always knew: the strict constraints of the paperweight form actually serve as a vehicle for some of the most exquisite and demanding displays of the glassmaker's art.

In the course of expanding our business we found ourselves discussing paperweights to an immense variety of people, from casual passersby at antique shows to knowledgeable and demanding collectors. From these experiences we began to see the need for a new kind of book: one that would serve as an introduction to collecting both antique and modern paperweights and as a guide to identification.

We've had the opportunity to travel widely and meet fascinating people, including collectors, dealers and artists. We've also had the satisfaction that comes with hard work and continual learning. We feel fortunate, indeed, to be associated with a field so full of beauty and with an infinite capacity for giving pleasure.

Lawrence H. Selman
Linda Pope-Selman
Santa Cruz, California
February, 1975

Fig. 1: A cranberry penholder rests atop a St. Louis crown paperweight.

Table of Contents

Introduction

Cavemen, having no paper, did not need paperweights. Actually it might be argued that modern man, despite the enormous piles of paper he uses and discards, *still* does not need *paperweights;* after all stones are readily available.

Indeed, we have a theory that paperweights, such as those defined in this book, were seldom, if ever, allowed to hold down paper. First created in the mid-nineteenth century by glass factories to show off their skill and entice prospective customers away from the competition, paperweights became a highly developed art form — collected even in their own time.

Serious investigation of this field did not appear, however, until around 1940 when Evangeline Bergstrom and Edgar Smith in America, and Imbert and Amic in France penned the opening paragraphs of the long tale of which this book is, for the moment, the latest installment.

The collecting of paperweights has been greatly encouraged of late by the Paperweight Renaissance of the last two decades. The art of quality paperweight manufacture, combining delicate craftsmanship and artistic sensibility with the effects of refracted light, is once again alive after a period of decline which lasted nearly a century. Lovers of this intricate art form may select from an impressive array of antique classics and modern classics-to-be in establishing and building collections.

It was to aid and abet these lovers, and perhaps kindle a few sparks in the hearts of the uninitiated, that this book was compiled.

Fig. 2: A Bigaglia perfume bottle with portrait canes.

Chapter I
How Paperweights Are Made

MILLEFIORI AND REPRESENTATIONAL GLASS PAPERWEIGHTS

The term "millefiori" means literally "thousand flowers." It refers to decorative glass manufactured by combining thinly-sliced cross-sections of fused bundles of glass rods of varying size, color, and shape, into vessels or ornamental pieces. The use of this technique in glass paperweights is antedated by the use of millefiori in bowls, knife handles, pen holders, seals, scent bottles (Fig. 2), and other glassware of Italian origin produced in the early 19th Century and, ultimately, by vessels utilizing millefiori canes from ancient Egypt and the Roman Empire. (Refer to Chapter II.)

The first step in creating a millefiori piece is to produce a wide variety of glass rods known as "canes." These are manufactured by rolling an iron rod, called a "pontil rod," over the surface of a pot of molten glass* (Fig. 3). The "gather" — the glass adhering to the pontil rod — is then shaped by rolling it over a flat plate made of iron or marble called a "marver" (Fig. 4). The first gather may be supplemented by subsequent dippings of the shaped glass into molten glass of other colors, thus forming a cane whose cross-section will be multicolored. Infinite variation in cane design is made possible through the use of molds (Fig. 5). The glass is pressed into a mold (Fig. 6). The resulting shape is shown in Fig. 7. Shaping tools and additional colors are also used to vary the design. When a cane is finished, a second pontil rod is attached to the other end of the cane (Fig. 8) which at this point may be a half foot long and three inches in diameter. Two workers then grasp the opposite pontil rods and move apart, stretching the cane out until it is as thin as a quarter of an inch (Fig. 9); the design, no matter how intricate, is preserved throughout the rod but has been miniaturized to the point where a tiny cross-section will seem the work of elves (Fig. 10). These simple rods, when cool, may be bundled together (Fig. 11) and reheated, to form a more complex cane.

---

*The basic ingredients of glass are ordinary sea sand, inorganic salts such as soda and potassium nitrate and, in the case of some crystal, lead oxide. Certain salts are added if a colored glass is desired, and the mix is heated until it is molten.

The ability to control the weight, color, feel, and allover effect of glass is a prerequisite for quality paperweight manufacture. The specific ingredients that go into a crystal or colored glass, and their proportions, are therefore "trade secrets."

Fig. 3

Fig. 4

Fig. 3: Taking a gather of molten glass. *Fig. 4:* Shaping the gather on the marver. *Fig. 5:* Molds used for millefiori canes. *Fig. 6:* Glass is pressed into a mold. *Fig. 7:* The shape after extraction from mold. *Fig. 8:* A second pontil rod is attached. *Fig. 9:* Cane is stretched until thin. *Fig. 10:* Miscellaneous canes by Charles Kaziun. *Fig. 11:* When cool, rods are bundled together.

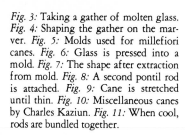

Fig. 5

Fig. 6

Fig. 7

Fig. 8

Fig. 9

Fig. 10

Fig. 11

The manufacturing techniques used in the fabrication of certain important types of millefiori canes are described in brief below:

Silhouette Canes: When the central gather of a millefiori cane is pressed in a mold shaped to represent a figure or emblem, the result is termed a "silhouette" cane; these canes and their classification are often crucial to the identification of a millefiori weight. It is common for the second gather — the contrasting layer surrounding the figure — to be pressed in a mold imparting a cogwheel shape. Examples of silhouette canes may be found in Chapter III.

Portrait Canes: Minutely detailed "pictures" can be achieved particularly well in canes composed of unmolded rods of various colors (See Fig. 2). Although these "portrait" canes were never used by the French, they were effectively utilized by early Italian glassmakers.

Lace or Upset Muslin: The underlying bed of "lace" or "upset muslin" on which the millefiori canes of many weights are arranged is made from the randomly placed fragments of a particular type of cane. These canes are created by positioning white glass rods at regular intervals around a central gather of clear glass. Then, during the pulling out, one pontil rod is twisted to create the spiraling white lines.

Latticinio: This term refers to a lacy backdrop also created from white and clear glass. Whereas "lace" is uniformly chaotic, latticinio is a basketweave creation of graceful regularity. The effect is created by laying white glass rods in a pattern over clear glass and blowing the mass into a bubble, which is then collapsed.

In this book, the term "representational paperweights" is used to identify those glass paperweights which enclose stylized representations of flowers, fruit, animals, reptiles, or similar objects, created by a glass artist using lamp-working techniques (Fig. 12). Representational weights may also contain millefiori canes. Paperweights containing plaques or cameo portraits of historical figures and those in which the glass covers but does not enclose a bas relief (Pinchbecks) are dealt with later in this chapter.

Once the decorative elements (canes or lampworked representations) have been created, they are arranged on a metal template (Fig. 13) and heated to just below the melting point (Fig. 14). This arrangement, surrounded by a "collar," is then "picked up" (Fig. 15) with a gather of clear or colored molten glass, which becomes the "ground" of the weight (Fig. 16). Grounds of many weights are convex upwards and are called "cushions." "Jasper grounds" are made by rolling the gather in a heap of ground glass of various colors before picking up canes or lampwork subject.

Further gathering creates the blob of crystal which, when appropriately blocked into shape (Fig. 17), becomes the "dome" of the weight. The shape of the dome is crucial to the refractory characteristics of the final product.

A neck is formed (Fig. 18) where the weight is then knocked off the pontil rod, leaving a characteristic bellybutton on the weight's base. This "pontil mark" (See Fig. 35) is usually removed with polishing and grinding. The annealing (cooling) process follows: this is a stage of the production process where many labor-intensive weights

Fig. 12

Fig. 13

Fig. 14

Fig. 16

Fig. 15

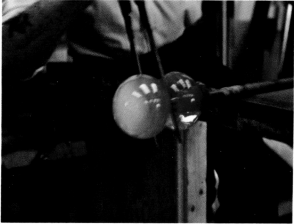

Fig. 18

Fig. 12: Creating lampwork flowers using a torch. Fig. 13: Arranging canes in a metal template. Fig. 14: The canes are heated. Fig. 15: Canes are surrounded by a "collar," then "picked up." Fig. 16: The weight is worked after canes have been picked up. Fig. 17: The glass is blocked, forming the dome. Fig. 18: The neck is formed.

Fig. 17

are lost. If the gathers of glass and/or the millefiori canes or lampwork subjects cool at different rates (due to incompatible composition of the different glass mixtures), the dome or the decorative elements will crack and the piece will be ruined.

SULPHIDE AND PINCHBECK PAPERWEIGHTS

In our description of the manufacture of sulphide paperweights, we defer to the Henry Ford of this craft, the lively and inventive Apsley Pellat who, in his famous and oft-quoted treatise, *The Curiosities of Glass Making,* writes:

> ". . . A Bohemian manufacturer first attempted to incrust in Glass, small figures of greyish clay. The experiments which he made, were in but few instances successful, in consequence of the clay not being adapted to combine completely with the Glass . . . The idea was caught by some French manufacturers, who, after having expended a considerable sum in the attempt, at length succeeded in incrusting several medallions of Buonaparte, which were sold at an enormous price. From the extreme difficulty of making these medallions, and from their almost invariably breaking while under the operation of cutting, very few were finished; and the manufacture was upon the point of being abandoned, when it was fortunately taken up by a French gentleman, Monsieur de St. Amans, who . . . prosecuted a series of experiments, by which, in a few years, he very considerably improved the invention . . .
>
> A patent was, some years since, taken out by Pellat for ornamental incrustations, called "Crystallo-Ceramie," which excited considerable notice at the time. By this process, ornaments of any description . . . are enclosed within the Glass, so as to become chemically imperishable. The substance of which these ornaments are composed, is less fusible than Glass; it is incapable of generating air, and at the same time is susceptible of contraction or expansion, as, in the course of manufacture, the Glass becomes hot or cold. It may previously be formed into any device or figure, by either moulding or modelling; and may be painted with metallic colors, which are fixed by exposure to a melting heat. These ornaments are introduced within the body of the Glass while the latter is hot, by which means the air is effectually excluded; the incrustation being thus actually incorporated in the Glass . . . The composition used in the patent incrustations is of a white silvery appearance, which has a superb effect when inclosed in richly-cut Glass."

Pinchbeck paperweights are mentioned here in order to differentiate them from the objects dealt with in later chapters of this book. They take their name from the surname of a watch and musical clockmaker of seventeenth century London. Pinchbeck is reputed to have developed a copper-zinc alloy closely resembling gold "in color, smell, and ductility." These weights and other similar objects fell under the shadow of the general cultural reproach of false gold which turned "pinchbeck" into a synonym for "counterfeit" or "spurious," or, more specifically, "costume jewelry." Modern collectors have begun to see redeeming qualities: the lively Pinchbecks had their heyday in the 1840's and 1850's, a point remote enough in time to make them respectably antique.

In Pinchbeck weights, unlike sulphides, the subject is not embedded in glass. The pinchbeck bas-relief plate is held by a base of copper, tin, alabaster or other substance, to which a glass lens is attached. The lenses were fabricated in much the same way as the domes of glass paperweights, though certainly not with the same care. The reliefs were probably manufactured through an embossing technique, whereby the design was impressed into a sheet of the metal. The motifs were based on religious, portrait, rural or Hellenic themes of popular sculpture.

Chapter II
A Brief History of Paperweight Manufacture During the Classical Period

Since its discovery glass has been used for both decorative and utilitarian purposes. The challenge of creating form and color from molten material has been the lifetime concern of countless glass craftsmen, most of them anonymous, a few of them justly celebrated.

Techniques ultimately used in the creation of classic glass paperweights were first developed and utilized in ancient Egypt — "before the exodus of the children of Israel from the land." The Egyptians manufactured practical necessities such as drinking vessels and vases, as well as mosaics and jewelry. The glass masters of the Nile strove to capture the color and shape of precious stones, and pioneered the enduring "millefiori" or "thousand flowers" technique. Transmitted and improved upon by the Romans, this technique has been further refined in the more modern art of paperweight manufacture.

The art of encasing millefiori canes, stylized glass flowers, and other figures and elements in clear crystal came to its zenith in the mid-nineteenth century. From approximately 1840 to 1870 European, and later American, artisans elevated the production into a dazzling and meticulous art. This Classical Period of paperweight creation was followed by a decline in the craft's worldwide volume and excellence, caused either by a change in popular taste or the refusal of craftsmen to pass down their techniques to succeeding generations.

French glassmakers are thought to have been introduced to the idea of paperweights as a saleable art form in 1845 at the Austrian Industrial Fair in Vienna, although some weights may have been manufactured previously in France. In Vienna, Pietro Bigaglia of Venice, one of a long line of Muranese glassworkers, displayed his wares* (See Fig. 2). It was once confidently surmised that Bigaglia's works were the catalyst for the subsequent development of sophisticated paperweight manufacturing techniques at the

---

*A few of those weights, bearing the initials "P.B.", have survived to our time. They are usually abstract in design, containing bits and pieces of colored glass rods and occasionally silhouette canes representing famous people, gondolas, or initials.

Fig. 19: **ANTIQUE BACCARAT PAPERWEIGHTS.** *Top row, No. 1,* Spaced millefiori on lace containing silhouette and date/signature cane; *No. 2,* Joan of Arc sulphide with side faceting and large flat top window. *Middle row, No. 3,* Camomile or pom-pom encircled by a ring of millefiori canes; *No. 4,* Top view of a mushroom with a close pack millefiori tuft. *Bottom row, No. 5,* A red primrose with white edging; *No. 6,* Pansy with bud.

Fig. 20: **ANTIQUE ST. LOUIS PAPERWEIGHTS.** *Top row, No. 1,* Crown weight; *No. 2,* Patterned millefiori on latticinio ground. *Middle row, No. 3,* Top view of a mushroom with a pink torsade; *No. 4,* Jasper panel weight with dancing devil silhouette. *Bottom row, No. 5,* A rare close concentric millefiori with one camel and seven dancing devil silhouettes, signed and dated; *No. 6,* Spaced millefiori on jasper ground.

13

three great glass houses of Baccarat, Clichy, and St. Louis. It was less than a year after the exhibition, however, that St. Louis and Baccarat were producing extremely fine weights, and, given the differences in quality and aesthetic detail between Bigaglia's early Venetian pieces and these earliest of classical French weights, it is hard to imagine how the French developed this skill in such a short span of time.

After about twenty years of creating these *pieces de résistance,* the three French giants yielded to the demand for lower-priced paperweights; fine quality work no longer seemed economically feasible. Paperweight production, always a relatively minor part of operations at Baccarat and St. Louis, was severely curtailed; and Clichy went out of business. Other European factories jumped in to supply the demand for low-quality novelty paperweights such as the "upright lily" and the "snowflake" varieties.

A great era was over in France, but paperweight-making had fortunately spread to England and America, where the tradition was kept alive for another twenty years before coming to the same inauspicious end. At the turn of the century a number of glassworkers in Millville, New Jersey, developed a footed upright rose (See Fig. 30, No. 3) and a few other new designs which they enclosed in well-constructed decorative weights — but this was a short-lived phenomenon.

Other than the early works of Paul Ysart and Charles Kaziun in the 1940's, it was not until the early 1950's that the art of paperweight-making was revived to any great extent. Individual artists in the United States and Scotland, as well as glass factories in France, England, and Scandinavia, began producing fine paperweights in the old French style or creating vital new techniques and motifs of their own. Today there are five glassworks and nearly a dozen individual craftspeople working in this area.

The foregoing notes on the general development of paperweight manufacture, and the more detailed accounts of the activities of the classic factories which follow, are placed at this point in our narrative in order to provide the reader with information requisite to an understanding of *"A Practical Guide to the Identification of Antique Glass Paperweights"* which follows in Chapter III. Before devoting a great deal of energy to identifying an antique glass paperweight, it is helpful to know a little about the factories which produced classical weights and why they were important. Though not intended to compete with or supersede much longer tracts on the same subject, the brief sketches below should give the reader a basic understanding of the historical development of glass paperweights.

Baccarat *(Fig. 19)*

Alsace-Lorraine, a much-disputed stretch of mountain and woodland, is located between the *Schwarzwald* (Black Forest) and the Vosges Mountains in northern France. It has been the home of the two greatest glass houses of France for over two centuries. The histories of Baccarat and St. Louis are intertwined with each other and with the sorry heritage of the wars which have crossed and recrossed this desirable territory from Charlemagne's division of Europe in the fifth century down to the global catastrophies of our century.

The company that today is called Compagnie des Cristalleries de Baccarat was founded as the Verrerie de Sainte Anne in 1764 by Monseigneur de Montmorency-Laval, a bishop. At that time its position on the right-hand bank of the Meurthe River was opposite to and outside of the hamlet of Baccarat, which has since grown to surround the factory site. The main purpose of the factory was the production of utilitarian glass for windows, mirrors, and bottles; nearby lumber resources recommended the location. The factory gradually grew into a little town: it was necessary for glass workers to live nearby and be ready to report for work at a moment's notice because of the unpredictability of the glass melt. One report states that, immediately prior to the French Revolution, the factory employed over 400 workers and that 70 families were housed on the factory grounds.

In 1819, a M. Aime Gabriel d'Artigues became the new owner of the Verrerie de Sainte Anne. He had worked for a time as director of the St. Louis factory and had operated his own glassworks in Vonneche, France until it was abruptly declared to be situated on Belgian territory in 1815. He subsequently purchased St. Anne for 2,845 ounces of fine gold, and transferred his fancy glass operations to that factory. The price was probably somewhat depressed, as the First Revolution and the Napoleonic Wars had made life for Verrerie de St. Anne hard: the price of new materials increased, the available labor force shrank, orders for a commodity that was still considered a luxury and was, in any event, vulnerable to cannon fire, dropped off. It was, in fact, only three years later that d'Artigues sold out and the firm adopted its present name.

The new management, headed by Pierre-Antoine Godard, led the factory rapidly into a position of pre-eminence among French glass houses. During the succeeding decades Baccarat exhibited frequently in Paris, winning a medal in 1823 and participating in the shows of 1827, 1834, 1839, 1844, 1849, 1855, 1867, and 1878. Like St. Louis, Baccarat did not send examples of their artistry across the channel to the Great London Exhibition in 1852, in which the British glass industry triumphed anew after struggling for a century with the Glass Tax.

Paperweight manufacture at Baccarat was a significant but small part of total production during the decade between 1845 and 1855. During the late 1960s paperweight production trailed off and almost 100 years elapsed before the art was revived.

St. Louis *(Figs. 20, 21, 22)*

Lorraine had been a center of "broad" glass manufacture for windows and mirrors for several centuries. It naturally became the focus of early eighteenth century efforts by the French to compete with high-quality glass being produced in other parts of Europe and England. Of the factories developed for this purpose, St. Louis was singled out for royal patronage. With this special encouragement, it went on to become one of France's leading glass houses. Its history closely resembles that of Baccarat, and the close connection and friendly competition of the two firms is symbolized even today by their contiguous facilities on the Rue de Paradis in Paris.

Fig. 21: **ANTIQUE ST. LOUIS PAPERWEIGHTS.** *Top row, No. 1,* Strawberry with bloom and two berries on latticinio ground; *No 2,* Nosegay or cane bouquet on an amber flash ground surrounded by a garland of canes. *Center, No. 3,* Concentric millefiori centered on a silhouette, dated in reverse SL-1848. *Bottom row, No. 4,* Mixed fruit in latticinio basket; *No. 5,* Patterned millefiori on latticinio.

Fig. 22: **ANTIQUE ST. LOUIS PAPERWEIGHTS.** *Top row, No. 1,* Unusual flat bouquet with waffle-cut base; *No. 2,* A scrambled or "end of day" weight. *Middle row, No. 3,* Faceted upright bouquet; *No 4,* Turnips on latticinio cushion. *Bottom row, No. 5,* Nosegay on an upset muslin ground; *No. 6,* Faceted nosegay.

Official recognition of the need to improve glass manufacturing techniques was first established in 1760 by the French Academy of Sciences, which offered a prize for the most successful suggestions. In 1772, the Academie adjudged a new lead glass developed by St. Louis to be equal in quality to the highly-valued flint glass of England. Earlier, in 1767, Louis XV had granted perpetual tax-free use of the St. Louis factory site to M. Rene-Francois Jolly and Company and the factory had been established as the Royal Glass Works of St. Louis. By 1788, with the manufacture of crystal now a major component of the factory's production, 637 persons lived around the glassworks in Munsthal.

M. d'Artigues, who founded his own glass factory at Voneche in 1800 and who subsequently owned the St. Anne (Baccarat) glassworks between 1819 and 1822, managed the St. Louis factory between 1791 and 1795. Almost as if it regarded d'Artigues' subsequent use of his knowledge of glass manufacturing techniques as a warning, the French State Council decreed in 1785 that a two-year prior notice was necessary for resignation from the St. Louis staff and that permission had to be obtained for travelling more than one mile from the factory! This decree reflected the prevailing attitude of governments toward the highly lucrative "trade secrets" of crystal production; indeed, the transmittal of sensitive technological information about glass was considered a major crime, punishable by death.

St. Louis introduced pressed glass into its product line in 1820, and in 1829 its growing specialization was recognized by a new firm name, Compagnie des Cristalleries de St. Louis. Two years later, in a joint agreement with Baccarat, St. Louis contracted with the retail firm of Launay, Hautin and Company, 50 Rue de Paradis Poissonniere, Paris, to sell their glass.

The correspondence between M. Launay and the St. Louis administration offers one of the rare glimpses available into the history of antique paperweight manufacture. M. Launay was full of ideas: he suggested inkstands, shot glasses, penholders, water glasses, and other domestic items as the appropriate recipients for millefiori decoration (See Fig. 1). He was certainly not one to mince words:

> "The fruit and flower weights you have sent us are awful. You cannot imagine the bad impression made by such merchandise, the surest way of stopping the selling of them is to go on sending us weights of that quality; the shape is poor, the filigree badly set, does not form the basket, the fruit is made anyhow; were they made by someone different from the workman usually in charge of them?"

Even when offering tentative praise, Launay was capable of causing management migraine:

> "Amongst those we have received from you we have chosen one which is a fine composition and which will sell well. This type is generally well made; but it is still necessary to look for a way to improve it so as to create as much lightness as possible in the composition of the bouquet. If we are returning it to you, it is so that you may notice how the white enamel flower detaches itself from the other colors. Return it to us as soon as you can and those which we will want from you will generally have the white flower."

The intrepid dealer's subtle blend of criticism and cajolery were an apparent success in the case of the fruit weights. After 1850, customers considered these to be among the best glass objects made at St. Louis.

St. Louis products were shown in many of the Paris exhibitions, but like their counterparts at Baccarat, the St. Louis management decided not to attend the Great London Exhibition of 1851, thus allowing Clichy to take top honors there. In 1867, St. Louis exhibited in Paris, but no mention is made of their paperweights; it is perhaps possible to conclude from this that the first era of paperweight-making at St. Louis had come to a close.

Clichy *(Figs. 23, 24)*

Because of the unfortunate destruction of most of the pertinent documents, the history of the third great French glass house of the Classic Period, Clichy-la-Garenne (sometimes called M. Maes, Clichy-la-Garenne), is gray from lack of detail and enlivened only by occasional chronological squabbles. Two possible founding dates are 1837 at Billancourt and 1838 at Sevres; the founders were Messrs. Rouyer and Maes. Shortly after its founding the firm moved to Clichy, now a Parisian suburb.

At first the factory made ordinary glass for export, but as early as 1844 they exhibited with Baccarat and St. Louis in Paris, where their colored and overlaid crystals were highly praised. Paperweights were a part of their product line displayed here, and apparently formed a part of a business stratagem designed to siphon off orders from the two more established glass factories. If Baccarat and St. Louis were not aware in their own right of the danger, they were soon informed of it by their perspicacious distributor in Paris, M. Launay, who wrote:

> "The selling of weights has now gone mostly to Clichy, which cannot fulfill all the orders received. This article (paperweights) has given a great importance to this factory by the contacts that were established through it with buyers who were not in the habit of applying there. Two furnaces are now permanently burning; a third one shall probably be lit up soon."

A stir was created in 1849 by Clichy's introduction at the Paris Exhibition of a new kind of glass, much lighter than traditional lead glass, but retaining the desirable optical properties of conventional crystal. Boracic acid was used as a flux in the manufacture of this type of glass. It came to be termed "boracic" glass. The judges were lavish in their praise and Clichy's star continued to climb during the next decade; as the only French factory to display their work at the London Exhibition of 1851, Clichy could only look good. In fact, their glass was so highly regarded in England that a number of English factories engaged Clichy workmen to set up production of similar glassware.

Clichy also participated in the New York Exhibition of the Industry of All Nations in 1853: the official catalog mentions Clichy in connection with a display of paperweights, perfume bottles, door knobs, etc. The factory continued to produce the show paperweights and related objects through 1870; after this year the quality of its products declined drastically. In 1885 the factory was taken over by a well-established glassworks in Sevres and paperweight production ceased forever.

Fig. 23: **ANTIQUE CLICHY PAPERWEIGHTS.** *Top row, No. 1,* Intertwined trefoil garlands centered on a white stardust and bull's-eye cane; *No. 2,* Spaced concentric millefiori with a central Clichy rose; *No. 3,* Open concentric millefiori on a lacy ground. *Middle row, No. 4,* Close pack millefiori in a stave basket; *No. 5,* Star garland millefiori centered on a Clichy rose; *No. 6,* A miniature swirl weight centered on a stardust cane. *Bottom row, No. 7,* Looping garland set in clear crystal; *No. 8,* A panel weight on a dark blue ground.

Fig. 24: **ANTIQUE CLICHY PAPERWEIGHTS.** *From top, clockwise, No. 1,* A rare pansy on a white latticinio ground; *No. 2,* A pink and white swirl centered on a moss green cane; *No. 3,* A rare turquoise mushroom double overlay; *No. 4,* A blue and white swirl centered on a complex geometric cane.

English Factories

The production of lead glass in England was burdened for a century by the Glass Excise Duty. Just or unjust, the levy was first imposed in 1745, then raised and gradually lowered until it ended in 1845. It had the effect of making it impossible for British glassmakers to compete with Bohemia, France, and Ireland in the market for crystal, because the tax was applied by weight.

Finally given an opportunity to experiment with glass for a profit, English glass houses began to imitate the millefiori designs already developed into an advanced art form by Baccarat, Clichy, St. Louis and other glass manufacturers on the Continent and to produce paperweights which were — gigantic! These magnum-sized weights, inkwells, and door-stops very likely represent an exuberant reaction against the days of repressive taxation.

London and Birmingham were the main centers of activity in the millefiori paperweight field.

BACCHUS: "Letter weights" were never more than a minute part of the total output at this Birmingham glassworks founded in 1818. Experimentation with millefiori techniques was part of a general attempt, following the repeal of the last sixpence of the glass tax, to recapture the domestic market in decorative glass from Bohemia and France. Attempts to imitate the *facon de Boême* led Bacchus to create a number of concentric millefiori weights which were subsequently praised by the *Art-Union Monthly Journal of the Arts* and the *Journal of Design and Manufactures* as being the equals of Continental production. In his *Encyclopedia of Glass Paperweights* (1969), Paul Hollister speculates that the number of paperweights produced by this factory is "probably no more than three or four hundred."

ISLINGTON: During the period that concerns us, the Islington Glass Works was owned by Rice Harris and Sons and shared the same economic conditions and geographic location as Bacchus. It is known that millefiori objects were displayed by them at the Exhibition of Manufactures and Art held in Birmingham in 1849, but no paperweights are listed in the catalog for that show. Of all the paperweights Islington may have made, two only are known.

WHITEFRIARS: A sector of London enjoying the right of religious sanctuary in medieval times, and subsequently famed as a haven for "debtors, cutpurses, highwaymen, and all the blackguards of the town," Whitefriars became the site of a glass house around 1860, which continued there until 1922. It began to produce millefiori paperweights (Fig. 25) around 1848 and has never stopped making them up to the present time. The family most consistently associated with the firm's ownership is the Powell clan. James Powell (1774-1840) moved from Bristol (where he had been a glass maker) to London in 1835 and purchased Whitefriars' glass plant. It was upon the death of the last Powell that the factory's operations were moved to their present location in Wealdstone, Middlesex.

The factory initially manufactured tableware such as decanters, drinking glasses, cruets, inkwells (Fig. 26), etc., primarily for export. Powell and Sons exhibited at the Great Exhibition of London in 1851 and at the Paris Exhibition of 1878; paperweights were presumably displayed on both occasions. The paperweights of the Powell era were characterized by the use of a concentric millefiori spacing scheme and similar motifs were used in other glass objects.

OTHER FACTORIES: Other factories not covered in detail here are those in the Yorkshire area which produced green bottleweights, or "dumps" as the English refer to them. The weights are discussed briefly in Chapter III.

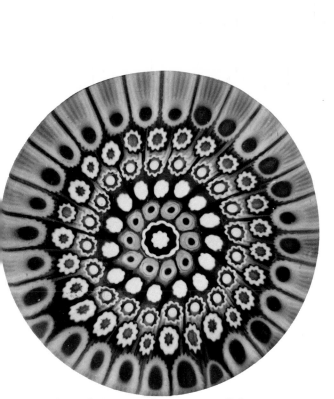

Fig. 25: Antique Whitefriars magnum millefiori.

Fig. 26: Antique Whitefriars millefiori inkwell. Note date in base.

Fig. 27: **ANTIQUE AMERICAN PAPERWEIGHTS.** *Top row, No. 1,* New England Glass Company nosegay surrounded by two millefiori garlands and resting on a latticinio ground; *No. 2,* N.E.G.C. hollow cane carpet ground. *Middle row, No. 3,* N.E.G.C. crown weight; *No. 4,* Sandwich or N.E.G.C. mixed fruit on latticinio. *Bottom row, No. 5,* Sandwich clematis with Lutz rose center; *No. 6,* Sandwich weedflower.

American Factories *(Fig. 27)*

Like many other developments that were transported from the Old World to the New during the seventeenth and eighteenth centuries, paperweight-making arrived in the United States a decade or so after its revival in Europe and lasted longer. It gradually became adapted to new economic and cultural climates; the production of relatively high-quality weights did not completely cease until after the turn of the century — long after paperweight manufacture had ended in France.

The first authentic dated American paperweight was produced by the New England Glass Company for the Great Exhibition of London in 1851 — an intaglio portrait of Victoria and Albert etched in a piece of clear crystal, not truly in the French tradition. The same company scored another first in the following year by issuing America's first French-style paperweight: a scrambled millefiori. The serious production of paperweights in large numbers, however, began only following the New York Exhibition of the Industry of All Nations, held in the U.S. Crystal Palace at Fifth Avenue and 42nd Street in 1853. American glass houses were quick to sense a favorable public reaction to the impressive exhibit of French weights, including some by Clichy written up by Horace Greeley.

American production, after a solely imitative beginning, branched off into its own specialties including an astounding array of lampwork subject weights.

The history of paperweight-making in America is better documented than that of production in France. Even the names of some individual glassworkers have been preserved. Three American glass houses stand out as producers of paperweights modelled on earlier French works: The New England Glass Company (N.E.G.C.) of East Cambridge, Mass.; the Boston and Sandwich Glass Company (Sandwich) at Sandwich on Cape Cod, Mass.; and the Mt. Washington Glass Works of South Boston and New Bedford, Mass. All three factories were founded by Deming Jarves, an enterprising Boston merchant. The three manufacturers also often drew on the same pool of skilled glass craftsmen, many of whom came from European apprenticeships, and even swapped millefiori rods (knowingly or unknowingly) on occasion. Thus, although each factory had a distinctive history, it is often difficult to distinguish the paperweights each produced.

THE NEW ENGLAND GLASS COMPANY: The NEGC was formed in 1818 around the nucleus of two defunct Cambridge, Massachusetts, firms — the Boston Porcelain and Glass Company and Emmet, Fisher and Flowers. Four partners, among them Deming Jarves who became general manager, incorporated in 1819 as the New England Glass Company of Lechmere Point, East Cambridge, Massachusetts. They set up a six-pot furnace and hired forty men for the production of high-quality flint glass. Scarcely a year later the factory was employing 80 men and 16 "youngsters" and producing $65,000 worth of glass per year. In 1850, the factory's work force had grown to 500 men working in round-the-clock shifts and output grossed $500,000 per annum. This was at the beginning of the plant's era of paperweight output, which extended from 1850 through 1880.

The 1870's brought the combined problems of labor unrest, increasing fuel costs and fiscal mismanagement. The firm was leased to William L. Libbey in 1878. He was later joined by his son as a partner in the firm. In 1888, the son closed down the New England plant in response to a strike and moved operations to Toledo, Ohio. The chief union organizer, Michael J..Owens went along, too; he was later to manage the new facility and to invent a revolutionary bottle-making device.

In 1856 the NEGC exhibited paperweights at the Franklin Institute's twenty-fifth exhibition in Philadelphia and at the Charitable Mechanics' Association exhibition in Mechanic's Hall in Boston where Sandwich also displayed paperweights. The inclusion of paperweights in the company's commercial displays indicates that they were not regarded as purely incidental "lunch-hour" production items. However, the history of NEGC paperweights is best told in terms of the few individual craftsmen who made them.

The first medallion weights produced in 1851 are associated with the Hopkins family. John Hopkins is said to have made millefiori weights around 1869 and his father is known to have been employed when the early intaglio weights were manufactured.

A family of glassmakers headed by Thomas Leighton (d. 1849) was employed by the NEGC. He had seven sons of whom William was the most creative: tradition has it that William created some of the highly prized double overlays produced by the factory.

The most notable name at Cambridge was Frank Pierre, a Frenchman who was apprenticed at Baccarat in his early teens and who came to work at NEGC at the age of fifteen, working there until his death at the age of thirty-eight. According to Mrs. Laura H. Watkins, author of *Cambridge Glass* and *American Glass and Glassmaking,* M. Pierre's health was not good, and he retreated to the tropics in the winter of each year with a group of glassblowers who "gave exhibitions" and enclosed ships and birds under the domes of their weights. Pierre made both millefiori and lampwork fruit weights in the French tradition, and was a great influence on paperweight making in America, particularly on the work of William Gillender.

SANDWICH GLASS COMPANY: (Fig. 28) Deming Jarves came into an inheritance of $25,000 in 1823, upon the death of his father. The ambitious "agent" or general manager of the glass operations at NEGC went to Pittsburgh to learn more about the manufacture of fine blown, pressed, cut and engraved glass. After observing the work of a number of glass factories in that area, he returned to Boston and severed his relationship with NEGC. He formed another glassworks, initially named the Sandwich Manufacturing Company. Upon the firm's incorporation in 1826, it was renamed the Boston and Sandwich Glass Company and Mr. Jarves became the general manager; he stayed with Sandwich for 33 years, until 1858.

Jarves' association with NEGC was the basis of much that happened subsequently at

Fig. 28

Fig. 29

Fig. 28: Sandwich double clematis. *Fig. 29:* Pairpoint compote. *Fig. 30:* MILLVILLE PAPERWEIGHTS. *L. to R., No. 1,* Footed weight with umbrella mushroom motif; *No. 2,* Inkwell with umbrella mushroom motif in bottom and in stopper; *No. 3,* Yellow rose attributed to Emil Larson.

Fig. 30

Sandwich: the know-how and manpower of the elder factory were drawn upon by its offshoot. Skilled men were also hired from the glass houses of England, France, Belgium, and Ireland. A friendly rivalry between NEGC and Sandwich, similar to that between Baccarat and St. Louis, became an important fact of life in the American glass industry and these two factories, along with famous glass houses in Pittsburgh, shared the limelight until their simultaneous closings in 1888. The growth of the Sandwich works paralleled that of Cambridge; records show that by 1854 the number of employees had risen from 70 to over 500 and the yearly output of glass increased from $75,000 to over $600,000. Price fixing arrangements were not unknown between the firms.

Much of the work of Nicholas Lutz, the most famous of all "American" glassworkers and paperweight-makers, is associated with Sandwich and with NEGC during a later period. Lutz was born in St. Louis, France, in 1834 — a propitious time and place for a career in paperweight manufacture. During his apprenticeship at the St. Louis factory, which he started at age ten, he may have helped in the early revival of millefiori techniques. He later travelled in Europe and worked at a number of glassworks, including Murano in Italy, thus obtaining a thorough background in glassworking and paperweight-making. As part of a group of seven glassblowers, he migrated to the U.S. in 1860; after stints in glass houses in Pennsylvania and New York and at NEGC (two years), he went to work at Sandwich, remaining there until the firm closed. He became well-known for his filigree glass, French style paperweights, and related objects; his flower and fruit weights were also extremely popular.

Timothy Collins, whom Jarves considered one of the most skillful workmen at Sandwich, also made paperweights — often presenting them to important customers and to officers of the firm.

MT. WASHINGTON GLASS COMPANY: Deming Jarves started yet another glass manufacturing operation in Sandwich in 1837, this time for his son George. The firm changed hands many times, however, becoming W. Libby and Company in 1870, Mt. Washington Glass Works again in 1876, a subsidiary of Pairpoint Manufacturing Company in 1894, the Gunderson Glass Works in 1938, and returning again to Pairpoint.

When Sandwich closed in 1888, Nicholas Lutz went to work at Mt. Washington and it is probably his influence that led workers to create beautiful magnum weights and paperweight plaques. These weights display a much different style than other contemporary American weights, however, and it is probable that Lutz himself did not create them.

While operating under the Pairpoint aegis, the factory made a number of footed weights and other objects containing a red and white spiral and fancy engraving on the foot. (Fig. 29)

GILLINDER: William T. Gillinder enjoyed a precocious rise to the top of the British glass industry, becoming at age twenty-eight the central secretary of the National Flint Glass Makers Society of Great Britain. He came to America after having been promised a job as gaffer of the main shop of the NEGC. His arrival in Massachusetts in 1854, however, was preceded by a business slump, and instead of the promised position, he was given one of less consequence. Catching the American version of *Wanderlust,* he moved about the country with his wife and children, working here and there, and making an abortive attempt to set up a glassworks in Baltimore, Maryland. At last, in 1861, he purchased an old bottle factory in Philadelphia and started what was first called Franklin Flint Glass Works, and which eventually became known as Gillinder and Sons.

The paperweights for which Gillinder is most noted are the commemorative ones issued as souvenirs at the Centennial Exposition in Philadelphia in 1876, where Gillinder and Sons set up the entire glass-making process in their own building. These souvenir weights included replicas of buildings at the exhibition and busts of Lincoln and Washington; they are not truly paperweights in the classical tradition. William himself, however, made a limited number of millefiori paperweights, and the establishment of this fact by Paul Hollister's sleuthing makes interesting reading *(The Encyclopedia of Glass Paperweights,* 1969).

MILLVILLE: Of the American paperweights made at the end of the nineteenth century, the most famous and most typically American are those which were manufactured in Millville, New Jersey. The factory with which the paperweight makers were associated was Whitall Tatum and Company.

Millville craftsmen did not so much imitate French paperweights as formulate a totally new and American statement in glass. A variety of paperweights and related objects were created: inkwells containing large, spotted, umbrella-like lilies (Fig. 30, No. 1); clipper ship profiles (Fig. 31) in powdered glass, and "devil's fire" patterns. The most famous product of this time and place was the "Millville Rose" (See Fig. 30, No. 3). This is a generic name for a group of crystal globes containing three-dimensional upright flowers — roses, tulips, and water lilies. Emil Stanger, Marcus Kunz, Ralph Barber, John Rhulander, and later, Emil Larson, were all associated with their manufacture. Like gardeners comparing their Helen Traubels with their neighbors' Red Beauties, Millville gaffers competed with one another to create the "perfect" blossom.

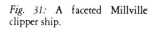
Fig. 31: A faceted Millville clipper ship.

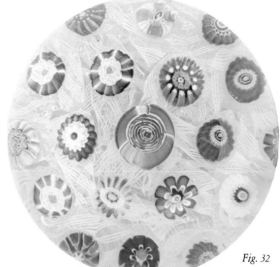

Fig. 32: Clichy spaced concentric millefiori signed with a "C" cane. *Fig. 33:*
Close-up detail of weight pictured in Fig. 32.

Fig. 32

Fig. 33.

Chapter III
A Practical Guide to the
Identification
of Antique Glass
Paperweights

The following section provides a general introduction to the key characteristics used in identification of antique glass paperweights. In addition it gives the collector a comprehensive, easily accessible reference for the more minute details of distinguishing, ascribing, and appraising paperweights.

Antique glass paperweights, like other classes of collectibles, vary considerably in value depending upon their design, workmanship, condition, and relative rarity. Paperweights created in the Classical Period (c. 1840-1870) and many contemporary editions made after 1950 are the most sought after pieces in today's market. There are, however, a great number of paperweights in existence that fall into the category of "decorative" weights. These weights tend not to increase in value over time, and are often — wittingly or unwittingly — marketed as appreciable antiques. Identification is thus a primary concern of any paperweight collector, novice or advanced. All collectors' quality modern paperweights are signed in one form or another.

IDENTIFICATION CANES FOUND IN
PAPERWEIGHTS DISCUSSED IN THIS
CHAPTER
1. Any date alone, if before 1900.
2. Any date, before 1900, in combination with signature B, SL or J.
3. Signature SL or C alone.
Refer to Chapter IV dealing with modern weights for identification of any paperweight having signature other than that shown above.

The information contained in this chapter will also be of use in identifying unsigned weights. The first section relates to the *general characteristics* of the weight. A second section deals with the construction, styling and spacing of *millefiori canes.* Subsequent sections are concerned with the *lampworked subjects, sulphides,* and *bottleweights.* Comparison of a weight's characteristics with those outlined here should lead to its identification. If none can be made there are two conclusions that may be drawn: 1. The weight is a "decorative" weight, a lovely keepsake, but not a valuable object d'art. 2. The weight is one of the peripheral types not covered in this book. These include the "upright lillies," common to Europe and the American midwest; the "snowstorm" novelty weights, which "snow" when turned upside down; advertising weights of any kind.

General Characteristics

BASES

Often the least glamorous part of a paperweight — the bottom surface most in touch with a rough and tumble world — will give clues to the quality and/or age of the piece. Both the way the base is finished and the pattern of scratches are key factors in weight identification. Four common types of paperweight bases are described in detail below.

Wear: This will be apparent on the bottom of a concave-based antique weight in the form of many uniformly distributed tiny scratches running in all directions forming a frosted ring (Fig. 34) on the part of the base which contacts the supporting surface. If scratches are long and sparse and only go in a few directions, start getting suspicious — these are warning signs of "instant aging." It should be recognized, however, that a good antique weight may show no wear at all. When a proud owner has the nicks or scratches polished out of the dome, the weight's base is often polished as well. Wear is only one factor to be weighed in judging the age of a paperweight.

Fig. 34: Frosted ring caused by wear.

Pontil Scar: As already mentioned in Chapter I, this term designates the mark left when a weight is broken off the pontil rod during fabrication. It is usually rough and sharp (Fig. 35), but sometimes appears in a smoother version, when it has been rough ground or slightly fire polished. The presence of a pontil mark usually indicates a weight of inferior quality, but there are exceptions. For example, the vast majority of the British green bottleweights have them, and some other English and later American types were left unfinished in this respect but are nevertheless collectible. If the subject of a pontil-marked weight is a tulip or crimp rose enclosed in clear glass, it may be a weight of the "Millville type." (Refer to section on American factories in Chapter II.) If the weight has a distinct ridge around the base where the dome and bottom were joined, you may have an English weight of value.

Fig. 35: Pontil scar.

Frosted Base: A translucent white base, created by grinding the bottom flat without final polishing, is referred to as a "frosted" base. Weights finished in this manner are usually of questionable quality and are not dealt with in this book. Certain collectible weights are finished in this manner, notably some by the Mt. Washington Glass Co.

Flat and Polished Base: This term denotes a weight bottom that is flat and bears a high polish. Most paperweights with flat polished bases are of newer vintage, and most of these are not fine collectors' pieces.

Concave and Polished Base: The pontil mark of almost all antique French and American paperweights was removed by grinding it smooth with a small convex wheel. The resulting concave bases were then polished to a high sheen. One interesting note is that the basal indentation is much shallower in a Sandwich weight than those made at the New England Glass Company.

Embellished Bases: Concave or flat polished paperweight bottoms often bear additional decoration. A particularly common ornament was a many-pointed star (Fig. 36), usually less than an inch in diameter, cut into the center of the base; viewed through the dome, this cutting appears to extend to the edges of the weight. Another star used in antique weights and still in use today is actually cut to the edges of the base. Other decorations present on both antique and contemporary weights are referred to as "strawberry-diamond," "waffle," or "grid" cuts (Fig. 37). (Refer to Glossary.)

PROFILES

Viewed from the side, characteristic paperweights from factories of the classic period reveal varying profiles. Sometimes this physical characteristic can be a factor in identifying a weight. However, we have found too many variations within a single factory to make this a reliable element in identification.

Fig. 36: Star-cut base.

TORSADE

The term refers to a large, opaque white ring of twisted lacy cane, around which a looser spiral of colored glass has been applied. It occurs only at the base of a weight, and may be accompanied by air rings above and/or below. Torsades are found almost exclusively in St. Louis and Baccarat weights. The direction of the colored spiral, when viewed from the side, is the distinguishing element; St. Louis torsades slant to the right, Baccarat to the left.

GROUNDS

The term "ground" refers to the background pattern or color upon which a paperweight's motif rests; grounds are most often present in the form of a lacy, latticinio, translucent or opaque colored glass cushion. Types of grounds include:

Colored: Background of colored glass, translucent or opaque; (See Fig. 23, No. 5)
Clear: Simply a gather of clear crystal;
Jasper: Ground glass particles of two colors; (Fig. 38)

Fig. 37: Grid cutting on base.

Latticinio: Criss-crossing swirls of white opaque glass strands: (Fig. 39)
Lace, Muslin or Upset Muslin: Fragments of filigree twists; (Fig. 40)
Carpet: Close-set identical millefiori canes. (See Fig. 27, No. 2)
Flash: Thin coating of translucent glass applied to weight's base (See Fig. 21, No. 2).

Certain grounds were used by some factories and not by others; consequently, the nature of a paperweight's ground can be a clue to its origin or age. The chart below attempts to draw some conclusions about the occurrence of types of grounds from a wide general experience with French and American paperweights — exceptions, however, may be found.

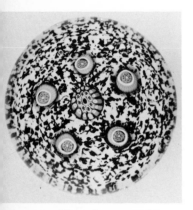

Fig. 38: Jasper ground.

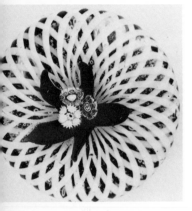

Fig. 39: Latticinio ground.

OCCURRENCE OF ANTIQUE GLASS PAPERWEIGHT GROUNDS

Yes = frequent occurrence   No = never occurs   Rare = infrequent occurrence

	Baccarat	Clichy	St. Louis	Sandwich	New England	Modern Italian	Chinese
Clear	Yes	Yes	Yes	Yes	Yes	Yes	Yes
Color	Rare	Yes	Rare	No	Rare	Yes	No
Jasper	Rare	No	Yes	Yes	?	No	?
Latticinio	No	Yes	Yes	Yes	Yes	Yes	Yes (coarse)
Lace or Muslin or Upset Muslin	Yes	Yes	Rare	No	No	Yes	Yes
Carpet	Yes	Yes	Yes	?	Yes	Yes	Yes
Sand	Yes	No	No	No	No	No	No
Flash	Rare	No	Yes	No	No	?	No

Fig. 40: Upset muslin ground.

GLASS CHARACTERISTICS

Weight: The paperweights of the Classical Period were for the most part made from glass of a high lead content. Clichy, however, introduced a boracic glass with characteristics similar to or better than crystal. Many of their weights are consequently lighter in heft. The glass used at Baccarat, St. Louis, and Whitefriars today contains as much lead as it did when antique weights were being manufactured; thus, these weights still seem heavy for their size. Perthshire of Scotland, like Clichy, has developed a glass for its modern weights with little or no lead which is very light but retains all the desirable optical properties of lead glass.

Clarity and brilliance are of the utmost importance in judging the quality of glasswork. The nature of the glass of the dome can rarely be the decisive factor in identifying an antique paperweight. Such qualities as the yellow cast characteristic of Chinese weights and the light weight of Italian glass, can help the collector distinguish old weights from new.

Imperfections: Bubbles, often created when the decorative elements of a paperweight are gathered into the glass dome, sugary appearance (striations) caused by uneven chemical composition within a batch of glass, and pieces of extraneous matter floating in the dome are all disagreeable imperfections from which no factory's weights are consistently free. They are not a significant aid in identification, though they may suppress a weight's value. Certain factories display consistent imperfections; Sandwich weights, for example, often have a "cowlick" at the apex of the dome where the glass was blocked.

FACETING

This term applies to the embellishment of the dome of a paperweight by grinding and polishing. Such external decoration can change the appearance of the internal motif, decreasing or increasing its apparent size or emphasizing something about it. The grinding of regularly spaced "windows" or punties or "printies" (terms used interchangeably to denote concave indentations around the dome) adds much interest to a paperweight. (Fig. 41) In the case of overlay weights, where clear domes are coated with one or more layers of opaque colored glass, these punties make it possible to see the subject within the weight. (Fig. 42)

Fig. 41: Faceted Baccarat primrose.

All factories faceted the top and sides of some of their weights, often grinding one facet atop the dome and five or six around the sides. In overlay weights, a sense of intimacy and mystery is created as the viewer peers through a tiny window at a decorative subject of seemingly magical craftsmanship surrounded by crystalline "air." In other types of weights, faceting multiplies the image or even, with overall faceting, makes it impossible to view the complete image. Thus the portrait of Queen Elizabeth II may be seen to approach and recede, twist, fragment, and revolve regally, as a 1953 St. Louis faceted paperweight commemorating her coronation is turned in the hand.

Fig. 42: Faceted Clichy double overlay.

Baccarat: The Baccarat factory often added a row of wide vertical flutes along the bottom of the weight to the usual scheme described above. Another effective Baccarat design features three concentric circles of small punties around the top window, covering the entire weight. Along with St. Louis, Baccarat sometimes used small diamond facets in overall cutting or combined these with larger windows. Large Baccarat sulphide weights usually have a large, flat top window and diamond faceting around the sides. (See Fig. 19, No. 2)

St. Louis: (Fig. 43) A popular St. Louis faceting scheme consisted of five or six large side windows and a circle of small oval windows around the top window.

Fig. 43: Faceted St. Louis nosegay.

New England Glass Company: The American firm used several faceting designs, among them a large top window concave with many small oval windows on the remaining overlay surface. Unique to this factory is quatrefoil cutting, featuring four overlapping windows, typical of NEGC paperweights, in both the rare overlays and the more common types. Two small rows of oval facets invariably accompany quatrefoil cutting on top of a weight.

Clichy: One particularly effective use of faceting by Clichy is an overlay which has only vertical flutes running along the weight's sides with a Clichy rose set at the intersection of the fluting on top.

Millefiori Canes

These minute glass rod cross-sections, the fabrication of which is described in Chapter I, are present in the majority of valuable antique glass paperweights, frequently appearing even when a lampworked motif is the center of attention.

PHYSICAL CHARACTERISTICS OF INDIVIDUAL MILLEFIORI CANES

Flaring: Millefiori canes manufactured by the Clichy factory characteristically flare at the base, producing a "skirted" effect. This characteristic was probably related to the relative temperatures of the arranged canes in the template and the molten glass with which they were gathered. The technique used in "picking up" the canes in the gather was probably also a factor.

Serrations: Viewed from the top, a number of canes appear to be edged with tiny cogs. The number of "cogs" in a typical cane varied from factory to factory and this makes for the relatively simple attribution of certain canes.

St. Louis canes, in particular, are easily identified using the "cog method." Their molds produced canes with 6, 7, and 14 points, along with other *multiples of seven.* Canes with 14 thin, long points were very popular and are frequently found (Fig. 44). The St. Louis silhouette canes are usually surrounded by a 28-pointed cog-wheel (Fig. 45).

All other factories seemed to favor canes with cogs numbering 5, 6, 8, and multiples of each. Cogs often adorn the outside perimeter of silhouette canes.

Cogwheel canes are still being used in paperweights, especially by Italian glassmakers. The canes appearing in these modern weights of modest value are characterized by large, coarse concentric cogwheels (Figs. 46, 47, 48), appearing most often in primary colors with generous use of white. Collectors can save themselves from making an expensive error by familiarizing themselves with this type of cane.

Following is a summary chart of cogwheel counts for various factories (Figs. 49, 50, 51, 52, 53, 54, 55, 56, 57).

GUIDE TO COGS OF MILLEFIORI CANES

Count	Origin
5 and multiples thereof	American, English, Modern Italian factories
6 and multiples thereof	Any factory
7 and multiples thereof	ONLY St. Louis
8 and multiples thereof	Any factory excluding St. Louis

Fig. 44

Fig. 45

Fig. 46

Fig. 47

Fig. 48

Fig. 49

Fig. 50

Fig. 51

Fig. 52

Fig. 53

Fig. 54

Fig. 55

Fig. 56

Fig. 57

Fig. 44: St. Louis cane with 14 points. *Fig. 45:* St. Louis serrated cane. *Fig. 46:* Typical Italian cane with coarse concentric cogwheels. *Fig. 47:* Typical modern Italian cane. *Fig. 48:* Modern Italian cane. *Fig. 49:* Clichy complex cane with bundled bull's-eye rods surrounded by 16 point cogwheel. *Fig. 50:* Typical Clichy 8 pointed cogwheel. *Fig. 51:* Antique American cogwheel cane with 10 points. *Fig. 52:* American cane with rods bearing 10 serrations. *Fig. 53:* Bohemian complex cane, cogwheel with 12 points. *Fig. 54:* Bohemian cane featuring cogwheel with 12 points. *Fig. 55,* Antique Whitefriars cane with 8 and 10 points. *Fig. 56:* Antique Whitefriars cane with 10 cogs. *Fig. 57:* Antique Baccarat silhouette cane with cogwheel shell.

37

DATE AND SIGNATURE CANES

The most straightforward way for a glass craftsman or a factory to "sign" a weight is to include in the weight an identifying millefiori cane. This was sometimes done in the Classical Period and is invariably the case with fine modern weights.

The presence of canes with numerals or letters on them may aid in identification; such canes can also be meant to mislead. The construction of an identification cane, the color scheme employed in its design, and the style of the letters or numerals themselves, must all be considered in determining the validity of a digital or initial cane.

The following chart lists valid dates, construction methods, and color schemes for all factories known to have used dated canes extensively.

	BACCARAT	ST. LOUIS	WHITEFRIARS (English)	SANDWICH OR NEGC (1)	BACCARAT-DUPONT	ITALIAN MURANO
Dates:	1846 1847 common 1848 most common 1849 1853 one only 1858 rare	1845 rare 1846 rare 1847 rare 1848 common 1849 rare	1848	1825 1852	1815 1837 1848 1851 1852 others	Many dates used; 1885 especially common
Cane Construction:	Numerals in individual fused rods. Initial B above most dates (2)	Numerals in individual fused rods. SL appears above all dated weights	Numerals in white rods separated by clear glass	Date set into an irregular-shaped cane	Numerals set in an oblong plaque or bar	A variety of date settings used; numerals seem to be handwritten
Color:	A combination of red, green and blue numerals in white canes	One color for numerals red, blue or black	All blue numerals in white canes	White numerals in blue canes most common	Black, green, red or blue numerals in a white bar	Usually black

1. New England Glass Company
2. The authors have seen one example where the date 1846 was in all white numerals surrounded by black. In addition, the date appeared to have been made of one rod rather than the usual 4.

The following sections describe in greater detail the use of date and signature canes by various factories and craftsmen.

Baccarat: Date canes appear in less than half the millefiori weights produced by Baccarat. Dates occurring in close-packed millefiori weights are 1846 through 1849, although there are instances of weights bearing the dates 1853 and 1858. The initial cane bears the letter "B" in red, blue, or green, most often embedded in a white cane. It is always accompanied by a date cane. (Fig. 58)

A number of color combinations for the four rods that comprise the date and initial canes have been observed. The typical date, B1848, for example, might show B in red, 1 in blue, 8 in green, 4 in blue, and 8 in green.

Fig. 58: Detail of Baccarat date cane.

Fig. 59: The Baccarat "church" weight.

Baccarat paperweights known to have date canes include the following types:

> Scrambled
> Close pack millefiori
> Scattered millefiori on lace
> Carpet grounds
> Chequer

A few of the more unique Baccarat items which are dated are worth noting. These include the well-publicized Baccarat "church weight," found in 1951 in the cornerstone of Baccarat's old church (Fig. 59); in the 1853 date cane the first two numerals are red and the other two blue; the letter B does not appear above the date. Weights made in commemoration of the visit of Marshal Francois Canrobert to Baccarat in 1858 are characterized by a large cogwheel cane in white bearing the inscription "Baccarat, 21 Avril 1858" above a laurel branch, rather than the usual rod type of date cane. This unique cane was placed in the center of a close packed millefiori design. There also exists a beautiful millefiori tazza (a shallow dish on a high thin pedestal used to hold wax seals), with the date 1846 worked into the design.

Spurious Dating of the Baccarat "Dupont" Weights: After the paperweight hey-day of the mid-1800's, a worker at the Baccarat factory named Dupont is said to have continued working independently. Weights attributed to Dupont are suggested to have been made as late as the 1930's. They sometimes contain date canes, ranging from 1815 to the mid 1850's. The most common types of weights attributed to Dupont are:

> Pansy
> Concentric millefiori
> Trefoil garland
> Patterned circlets of millefiori
> Heart-shaped patterns

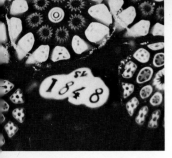

Fig. 60: St. Louis date/signature cane.

Fig. 61: St. Louis signature cane.

Fig. 62: Clichy signature cane with serif.

Fig. 63: Clichy signature cane with serif.

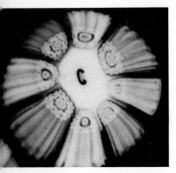

Fig. 64: Clichy signature cane, sans-serif.

Dates, when present, occur in black, red, green, or blue in a white bar; they are located in the center of a motif or near the bottom of a pansy. The dating of a pansy, incidentally, violates the general rule that antique flower weights do not contain date canes.

Saint Louis: Far fewer signed and dated paperweights were made at St. Louis than at Baccarat. Their date/signature canes, made of numeral and initial rods, are usually smaller, though similar in construction. Appearing in one color — either red, blue, or black — these dates always occur with the factory initials "SL" above the date (Fig. 60); occasionally the cane will appear backwards because of upside-down placement in the design. It is interesting to note that in many St. Louis weights where a date cane occurs, the symmetry is disturbed and the circles of millefiori canes made irregular by the addition of the identification cane.

Signature/date canes have been recorded in the following types of antique St. Louis paperweights:

Carpet ground	Piedouche
Close concentric	Scrambled
Mushroom	

St. Louis initial canes, unlike the Baccarat initial, are sometimes found without an accompanying date (Fig. 61). They then appear as a large cane set in close concentric millefiori weights or in a few scrambled pieces.

Clichy: There are no recorded instances of date canes appearing in Clichy weights. Clichy, however, is the only factory known to have made a cane where the company name appears in full; this extremely rare cane has been found in the bottom of a moss-green carpet ground weight and in a pair of millefiori vases. Fragments of the signature are sometimes found in scrambled weights. (See Fig. 65)

The Clichy initial "C" cane occurs more frequently. Red, blue, green, or black initials are found in two styles — serif (Fig. 62) (Fig. 63) and sans-serif (Fig. 64). The letter appears in the center of a variety of pastry mold canes.

A variation of the Clichy signature appears in the semicircular garland weights in which five or six C-scroll garlands of millefiori florets are placed open-side-inward around two or three concentric rings of canes (Fig. 66); these weights were produced in many cane and color combinations and may be considered to be signed.

Initial "C" canes have thus far been observed in the following types of Clichy paperweights (Fig. 67):

Barber pole chequer	Piedouche
Carpet ground	Patterned millefiori
Chequer	Scrambled millefiori
Close pack millefiori	Spaced millefiori
Panel	

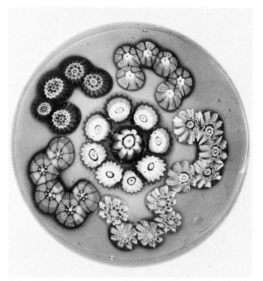

Fig. 65: Clichy scrambled weight with signature cane.

Fig. 66: Clichy patterned millefiori with C-scroll garlands.

Fig. 67: **SIGNED CLICHY WEIGHTS.** *Top, No. 1,* Chequer weight. *Left, No. 2,* Spaced millefiori on lace. *Right, No. 3,* Spaced millefiori on rare translucent cranberry ground.

Fig. 68: Whitefriars date canes, 1848.

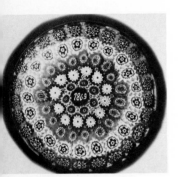

Fig. 69: Modern Italian millefiori, false date.

Fig. 70: Modern Italian date cane, 1885.

Fig. 71: Modern Italian date cane, 1869.

Whitefriars: The only date known to appear in antique Whitefriars millefiori work is 1848 (Fig. 68). It is composed of rather crude blue numerals, each enclosed in a separate white cane. The number 4 looks like a backwards f, while the 8, upon closer inspection, resembles two dots placed one above the other. The canes bearing the numbers are often askew, making the date difficult to read. Whitefriars dates occur in inkwells, newel posts, door-stops, and in the outer ring of concentric millefiori paperweights. (A discussion of modern Whitefriars identification canes, and those of other factories, follows in Chapter IV.)

Sandwich: The dates 1825 and 1852, the only ones used by Sandwich, appear only in their scrambled millefiori weights. There is an hypothesis that the 1825 canes may actually be 1852 canes with the last two digits reversed; a more likely theory, however, is that the earlier date commemorates the founding of the Sandwich glassworks. One collector/musician highly prizes his Sandwich scrambled weight in which several 1852 date canes are included.

Bohemian: In several Bohemian paperweights featuring scattered millefiori on lace, a single date cane reading 1848 has been observed; white numerals in colored glass, sometimes with the initial "j" above, comprise the date cane. The meaning of the letter "j" has not yet been definitively determined; various paperweight specialists have speculated that the "j" stands for the Josephice glass works, for a craftsman's initial, or for the word *jahr* (German for "year" or "date").

Murano: (Fig. 69) Fake dates are found in various settings in Italian weights; a variety of dates are used, but 1885 seems most common. (Fig. 70, Fig. 71) The digits are most often black on a white ground and have a crude handwritten appearance. In recent years we have seen many modern Italian weights bearing an acid etched stamp of a decanter, goblet and tumbler enclosed in a circle, similar to the Baccarat logo. This spurious signature stamp is somewhat larger and etched deeper into the glass than the authentic Baccarat mark it imitates.

Sulphides: The dating of antique sulphide cameos is rare, but there are examples. One is a famous commemorative weight made for the Crystal Palace Exhibition of 1851 by the New England Glass Company (NEGC), which is probably the first classic paperweight manufactured in the U.S. Another is a sulphide of Lajos Kossuth, dated 1851 and bearing the inscription: "Ex-Governor of Hungaria/Set At Liberty By The American People." It was probably manufactured at either NEGC or Clichy.

Only a small percentage of sulphide cameos are signed on the back; this was accomplished either through impression or printing. English signatures include:

Apsley Pellatt	Allen and Moore
Patented in London	A and M
Pellatt and Green	

Those cameos produced in Scotland by John Ford are sometimes signed Wood, or L. C. Wyon. Among the French signatures are:

Deprez	Acloque, fils.
D. P.	Feuillet
Dihl	Martoret
Montcenic	C. A.
Schmidt	P. D.

Additionally, the name Andrieu is found pressed on the bottom of the bust of a number of French sulphide elements; Andrieu was a master engraver and medallist from whose works these cameos were taken. It should be noted that occasionally the name of the subject was written on the back of the sulphide. (Fig. 72) This of course should not be confused with the manufacturer.

Fig. 72: Sulphide back with identification of subject.

SILHOUETTE CANES

After signature and date canes, millefiori most attributable to a particular factory are the "silhouette canes." They are so named because their cross-sections bear the likeness of minute animals, plants, or human figures in profile. Even the best renderings are necessarily simplistic and childlike, and this is perhaps what makes the silhouettes seem a trifle alienated from their intricate environment: against the completely abstract backdrop of a close pack millefiori paperweight, for example, silhouette canes stand out dramatically highlighted, as if they were meant to be whimsical reminders of childhood.

Silhouette canes are crucial to paperweight identification because they varied so distinctively and consistently between manufacturers of antique glass paperweights. The idiosyncrasies of silhouette handling are discussed in depth below.

Baccarat: Baccarat excelled in the production of silhouette canes. The figures are either red, white, dark blue, or black; the glass immediately surrounding them is of a contrasting color, usually white, dark blue, or black; the outer casing, often shaped into a cogwheel, may appear in a number of colors.

One of the most beautiful of all silhouettes produced at Baccarat is the swan (Fig. 88): a white swan swims on azure "water" surrounded on the top and sides by a shell of thirteen salmon-colored rods; below are placed three turquoise honeycomb canes.

Of the twenty or so canes present in a typical Baccarat paperweight featuring scattered millefiori on lace, seven might be silhouettes. A miniature may have four silhouettes out of seven canes. Close packed millefiori weights with as many as 24 silhouettes and as few as one have been recorded. Silhouette canes were frequently utilized in trefoils, mushrooms, overlays, carpet grounds, and the rare chequer weights.

Fig. 73: Red devil.

Fig. 74: Squirrel.

Fig. 75: Love birds.

Fig. 76: Pelican.

Here is a list of subjects used by Baccarat in their silhouette canes in antique weights: (Figs. 73, 74, 75, 76, 77, 78, 79, 80, 81, 82, 83, 84, 85, 86, 87, 88)

Red devil	Black monkey
Squirrel	Butterfly
Love birds	Double flower
Pelican	Single flower
Pigeon	Horse
Rooster	(not shown)
Deer	White monkey
Dog	Pheasant
Goat	Stork
Elephant	Man with rifle

We have mentioned above that silhouette canes, because of technical limitations and size, are "necessarily simplistic and childlike." Another reason for the naive charm of Baccarat silhouettes is that they were actually based on designs created by a child. Joseph Emile Gridel, the nine-year-old nephew of Baccarat manager Jean-Baptiste Toussaint, set out in 1847 on a simple project — he cut out 18 different animals he had drawn and was pasting them onto paper when his uncle spotted them. The cut-out designs eventually became models for silhouette cane molds and, in 1848, M. Toussaint was able to give his budding young artist a paperweight containing fifteen of the animals as a reward for supplying the drawings; the weight is still in the possession of the Gridel family.

In 1971 Baccarat embarked on a new line of paperweights based on the Gridel designs and called the "Gridel Series." Each of the weights, which are being produced in a series of limited editions, features a large central version of one of the silhouette canes, surrounded by the complete set of 18 in smaller size. The design is complemented by concentric rows of geometric millefiori and by a cushion of lace. A listing of the weights issued thus far is included in Chapter IV; the series is mentioned here simply to make paperweight identifiers immediately aware of its existence and to prevent confusion.

Fig. 77: Pigeon.

Fig. 78: Rooster.

Fig. 79: Deer.

Fig. 80: Dog.

Fig. 88: Close-up of Baccarat swan cane.

Fig. 81: Goat.

Fig. 82: Elephant.

Fig. 83: Black Monkey.

Fig. 84: Butterfly.

Fig. 85: Double flower.

Fig. 86: Single flower.

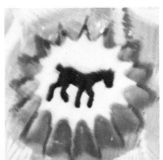

Fig. 87: Horse.

Clichy: No known examples of a Clichy weight containing silhouettes are extant and thus this factory may be eliminated as a possible origin of a weight with silhouette canes.

St. Louis: Although not an integral element in paperweight design at St. Louis as it was at Baccarat, silhouette canes — and some very interesting ones — are found in St. Louis scrambled and carpet ground millefiori paperweights. One scrambled weight contains a silhouette cane portraying a man standing atop a dog. Following is a list of St. Louis silhouette cane motifs. (Figs. 89, 90, 91, 92, 93):

Dancing couple	(not shown)
Dancing lady	Dog
Dancing man	Dog with rider
Dancing devil(s)	Duck with duckling
Camel	Turkey
	Flowers

Bohemian Silhouette Motifs: These included the following (Figs. 94, 95):

Striped bee	
Dancing devils	Monkey
(not shown)	Running rabbit
Devil	Eagle
Dog	Horse

American Silhouettes: Paperweights manufactured by NEGC and Sandwich occasionally feature silhouette canes, particularly in scrambled millefiori weights. Some carpet grounds utilize a silhouette cane as a central motif: one weight in the collection on display at the Stourbridge Village Museum in Massachusetts contains a running rabbit silhouette cane as the central subject on a concentric hollow-cane carpet ground. Another amazing example contains 83 minute rabbit silhouettes, hidden in a concentric millefiori design.

Silhouette subjects found in American weights include (Figs. 96, 97, 98)

Eagle	(not shown)
Heart	Bee
Running rabbit	Dog

English Silhouettes: Of the British glass paperweight manufacturers, only Bacchus is known to have used a silhouette cane . . . the profile of an unidentified woman used as the central cane in some concentric designs.

GEOMETRIC CANES

In addition to checking for date/signature and silhouette canes, a collector can find further clues to a millefiori weight's identity by studying the geometric canes.

Some of these are unique to a single factory; more often, a particular cane pattern was used by several factories but handled differently by each. A knowledge of these

Fig. 89: Dancing couple.

Fig. 90: Dancing lady.

Fig. 91: Dancing man.

Fig. 92: Dancing devils.

Fig. 93: Camel.

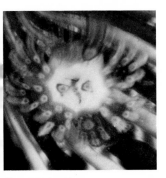

Fig. 94: Striped bee.

Fig. 95: Dancing devils.

Fig. 96: Silhouette of eagle surrounded by running rabbits.

Fig. 97: Silhouette of heart.

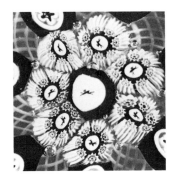

Fig. 98: Silhouette of running rabbit.

Fig. 99: Clichy rose cane.

Fig. 100: This weight is easily identified by its millefiori canes.

Fig. 101: American version of Clichy rose cane.

Fig. 102: Modern Italian rose cane.

Fig. 103: Baccarat stardust cane, bulls-eye center.

Fig. 104: Clichy moss green cane.

Fig. 105: Clichy moss green canes.

Fig. 106: Clichy edelweiss cane.

idiosyncratic cane features will occasionally permit identification of an otherwise unidentifiable weight.

Rose Canes: The "Clichy rose" must be the best known geometric millefiori cane (Fig. 99). Composed of concentrically arranged flattened glass tubes centered on a stamen-like ring of tiny round yellow rods, this cane more closely resembles a slice of rosebud than a full bloom. The perimeter of the blossom is usually complemented by a circle of vertical staves of a contrasting color. Pink Clichy roses with green staves are most commonly found, but many color combinations have been observed: white, turquoise, amethyst and, rarely, yellow roses were used with various stave colors.

A rose cane was also made in the United States during the Classical Period, reportedly by Nicholas Lutz at Sandwich. This type (Fig. 101) always features a solidly-colored center rod, but is similar in other respects to the Clichy rose. It was used primarily as a center in poinsettia weights.

The Muranese manufacture just about everything in glass, including millefiori canes resembling roses (Fig. 102). But their primitive interpretation of this motif should not be mistaken for the authentic and elegant Clichy specimen.

Bohemian millefiori weights occasionally contained another version of the rose cane similar to that of Clichy. The distinguishing trait of this cane, known only in pink, is the wider spacing of the flattened "petal" rods. The overall effect is less delicate than the authentic Clichy.

For a detailed analysis of rose canes see 'Roses, Roses' by Don Eckles in the 1974 *Bulletin of the Paperweight Collectors' Association.*

Stardust: The cane is composed of circles of tiny white, star-shaped rods separated by clear glass and surrounding a red or green whorl or bulls-eye cane. It is an appealing combination that was used extensively by all French factories during the Classical Period (Fig. 103). The only real distinction that can be drawn between the stardust canes of various glass establishments is the tendency, discussed previously, for the Clichy canes to flare at the base.

Moss Green: These canes (Figs. 104, 105) represent a simple but subtly beautiful use of the "bundled rod" technique of millefiori manufacture and are uniquely Clichy's. Massed together they provide a deep and restful background for patterned millefiori motifs.

Edelweiss: A cane resembling the Swiss national flower with its minute colored stamens, gives this unique Clichy cane its name (Fig. 106). A veil of bubbles sometimes surrounds this cane.

Fig. 107: Baccarat arrow cane.

Fig. 108: Baccarat arrow cane.

Fig. 109, St. Louis arrow cane.

Fig. 110: Baccarat arrow canes around central star rod.

Fig. 111: Baccarat cane with cylindrical honeycomb rods.

Fig. 112: Baccarat star honeycomb cane.

Fig. 113: Baccarat stardust cane with bulls-eye rod.

Fig. 114: Baccarat shamrock cane.

Fig. 115: St. Louis star rods, serrated tubular casing.

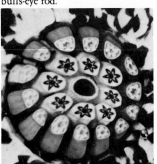

Fig. 116: St. Louis complex cane with star rods.

Fig. 117: Baccarat star cane.

Fig. 118: St. Louis hollow cane with 14 serrations.

Arrow or Crowsfoot Canes: This three-pronged pattern was used by all three French factories in wedge-shaped serrated canes. The variations on this theme are: Baccarat — prongs are straight lines (Figs. 107, 108); St. Louis — outer prongs are curved, resulting in an anchor-like motif (Fig. 109); Clichy — similar to St. Louis but thicker. Frequently arrow canes were grouped around a central star-shaped rod (Fig. 110); however, other centers were also used. In a design variation unique to Baccarat, simple arrow rods form the lower petals of a pansy (See Fig. 162).

Honeycomb: This motif was used only by Baccarat. Resembling its natural counterpart, the honeycomb cane is constructed from transparent cylindrical or star-shaped rods surrounded by opaque glass, bundled and fused to form the characteristic honeycomb pattern (Figs. 111, 112). Honeycomb canes occur at the base of the Baccarat swan silhouette (See Fig. 88).

Whorls ("Jelly Rolls"): A version of this cane has been used in millefiori decoration since Egyptian times. All of the French factories utilized it.

Bulls-Eye: These minute "targets" were most commonly bundled together with other rods to form a complex cane. Employed by all factories, they were popular at Baccarat as a central rod for stardust canes. (Fig. 113). See also Fig. 49 for a grouping of Clichy bulls-eye rod used in a complex cane.

Shamrock: The Irish symbol was used exclusively by Baccarat, usually composed of dark glass embedded in an opaque white glass rod (Fig. 114).

Star: Another silhouette-type rod in dark colors on white grounds, the six-pointed star serves as the center for a variety of complex canes (Figs. 115, 116, 117). It was used primarily by Baccarat.

Hollow or Tubular: The center of these millefiori are not really hollow — they are composed of a clear glass gather. They are often surrounded by a cogwheel with 10 serrations, (Sandwich, NEGC) or 14 serrations (St. Louis) (Fig. 118). See section on *Serrations,* page 36.

Random Spacing Schemes

Antique glass paperweights are often classified according to the arrangement of the millefiori canes within them. Although internal spacing seldom yields positive proof of a weight's date or origin, it is a factor on which the rarity of a particular item is often determined. Sometimes a particular spacing scheme forms the basis for a specialized paperweight collection.

SCRAMBLED MILLEFIORI OR MACEDOINE: The most common of all antique paperweights are the scrambled millefiori (Fig. 119). The term "macedoine," or scrambled lace, is applied to scrambled weights composed largely of fragments of lacy twists. Many intriguing hours can be spent with a magnifying lens and one of these jumbled arrays of the leftovers of the gaffer's art. Exciting discoveries are possible: perhaps a minute silhouette will pop up unexpectedly, or a lacy twist worthy of the rarest paper-

Fig. 119: **ASSORTED SCRAMBLED WEIGHTS.** *Top row, No. 1,* American. *No. 2,* Clichy. *Center, No. 3,* St. Louis. *Bottom row, No. 4,* Chinese; *No. 5,* Baccarat.

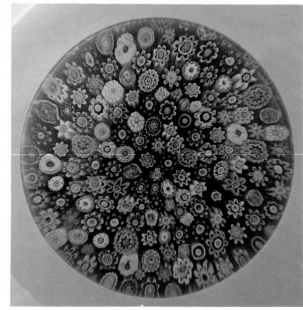

Fig. 120: Clichy close pack millefiori.

Fig. 121: **ANTIQUE MILLEFIORI PAPERWEIGHTS.** *Top row, No. 1,* Clichy trefoil garland with two roses, set in clear crystal; *No. 2,* St. Louis crown; *No. 3,* N.E.G.C. close concentric millefiori. *Middle row, No. 4,* Baccarat close pack millefiori with silhouettes and date/signature cane; *No. 5,* Clichy panel weight on opaque white ground; *No. 6,* Baccarat open concentric with central arrow cane. *Bottom row, No. 7,* St. Louis nosegay; *No. 8,* Whitefriars magnum concentric with date 1848; *No. 9,* St. Louis mushroom with concentric millefiori tuft.

weight will come to light. Only infrequently will a scrambled paperweight contain signature or date canes. Unsigned examples may be acquired for a relatively small cost, while affording the novice collector a good introduction to antique paperweights.

Clichy: Most colorful of all scrambled paperweights are those made by Clichy: small "C" initial canes and fallen petals from Clichy roses lurk here. The lucky collector may also find part or all of the rare "Clichy" signature cane hidden somewhere in a twisted millefiori jungle.

Baccarat: The Baccarat macedoines are very light and lacy in appearance. They are made up of short opaque and lacy twists in blue, green, and red, set at right angles. Relatively few Baccarat macedoines are extant. One Baccarat scrambled weight, dated 1847, is composed entirely of silhouette cane fragments.

St. Louis: Pistachio and salmon colors and unique, sharp-pointed canes are typical of the St. Louis macedoine paperweights. Occasionally a SL signature cane or a silhouette may be included, much to the collector's delight.

American: Affectionately termed "candy cane" or "broken candy" weights, American macedoines display all the variety of color and form to be found in a dozen confectioneries. Some are sparsely filled with pastel-colored canes and lace; others take on a dark appearance and are fully packed with both whole and broken canes. Rabbit, heart, and eagle silhouettes and occasionally a cane dated 1852 are found.

CLOSE PACK MILLEFIORI: Not quite as chaotic, but just as intricate, as the scrambled weights are the "close pack millefiori" weights featuring a random assortment of canes packed tightly together in an upright position to form an overall design.

Baccarat: The close pack spacing scheme was the basis of some of Baccarat's most successful paperweights (Fig. 122 also see Fig. 121, No. 4). The florets often rest on a cushion of lace, usually visible only from below. Canes in the outer row are longer than the rest and are frequently pulled under the weight to give it a finished appearance. Baccarat close packs vary in size from miniatures to a recorded example of over four inches in diameter.

St. Louis and Clichy (Fig. 120) apparently left major production of close pack millefiori weights to Baccarat, although some examples are known. A modern Italian example (Fig. 123) is shown for the basis of comparison.

Patterned Spacing Schemes

CONCENTRIC PAPERWEIGHTS: When a millefiori paperweight's motif is based on a number of concentric circles enclosed within each other, it is said to be a "concentric" weight. "Looking at a good concentric," writes Paul Hollister, "one feels that this is what paperweights were meant to be." The conformance of design motif to the overall shape of the paperweight takes an observer's mind off distracting patterns and allows attention to be focused on the order and design of individual millefiori canes.

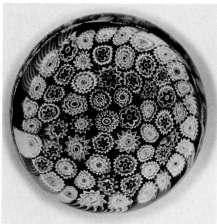

Fig. 122: (above) Baccarat close pack millefiori. Signed and dated b 1848. *Fig. 123: (left)* Modern Italian close pack milefiori. Compare cane construction with weight above.

Fig. 124: Clichy spaced millefiori on lace.

Fig. 125: Baccarat spaced millefiori with silhouette canes and date B-1847.

Fig. 126: St. Louis spaced millefiori on jasper ground.

Fig. 127: St. Louis spaced millefiori with ring of canes.

Fig. 128: Clichy chequer with rare yellow rose.

Fig. 129: Modern Italian chequer weight.

SPACED MILLEFIORI: This term denotes a design scheme in which individual millefiori florets are set at equal or nearly-equal distances apart, thus forming a set of vaguely defined concentric circles. The design was often slightly botched in production, the canes being set at irregular intervals; hence the more common appellation "scattered millefiori." Weights in this category occur on a variety of grounds and were manufactured by all three of the classic French factories.

Clichy: (See Fig. 23, No. 2) More spaced millefiori paperweights have been ascribed to Clichy than to any other factory; this was, indeed, a pattern in which M. Maes specialized. Grounds used were usually either clear or colored or filigree "lace" — the latter type are commonly referred to as "scattered millefiori on lace." The Clichy rose will often appear in this setting, with one or more roses interspersed with other types of canes; in rare instances a signature cane is also included (Fig. 124).

Baccarat: Baccarat usually provided a backdrop of lace or upset muslin for its spaced millefiori paperweights, often placing a butterfly silhouette cane in the center of the design. (Fig. 125, also see Fig. 19, No. 1) Date canes are another frequent feature: the date will be either 1846, 1847, 1848, or 1849, with 1848 being most common. Baccarat scattered millefiori weights range in size from miniature to magnum. Unique to Baccarat is the rare spaced millefiori weight which features large, attractively bold canes with shamrock silhouettes. This large weight with its upset muslin ground is a collector's delight.

St. Louis: The simplest type of St. Louis spaced millefiori contains five florets about a central complex cane. A variety of grounds were used to support this spacing design typical of St. Louis. They are: clear, jasper (Figs. 126, 127), lacy, swirling latticinio (See Fig. 21, No. 5), and, in some rare cases, colored grounds. An abbreviated form of this motif, consisting of only one complex cane, is sometimes featured with a jasper cushion.

CHEQUER WEIGHTS: One variation of the spaced millefiori design which must have been popular, if only because so many fine examples are extant, is the "chequer weight." Made principally by Clichy (Fig. 128), this scattered millefiori on lace design featured short lengths of latticinio twists used to define rectangles around the spaced canes, giving the entire weight a checkerboard look. Where colored twists were also utilized to divide up the "board," the resulting motif is called a "barber pole chequer."

Only two chequer weights are known to have been made at Baccarat. These examples contain long strips of opaque rods dividing the spaced millefiori. Both examples contain date and silhouette canes.

Glass workers in Italy, too, have tried their hand at a chequer weight. Their coarse rendition is shown in Fig. 129. Note the typical modern Italian millefiori canes.

CARPET GROUND SPACED MILLEFIORI WEIGHTS: The antique spaced millefiori paperweights of greatest value are those set against a solid background of identical millefiori canes — the carpet ground (Fig. 130). St. Louis, for example, used carpet

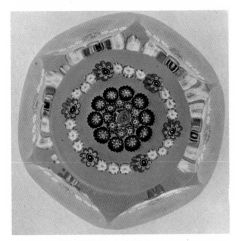

Fig. 131: Faceted Clichy open concentric.

Fig. 130: Baccarat carpet ground spaced millefiori.

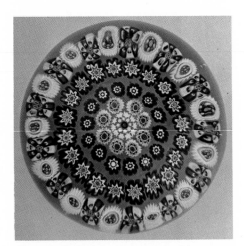

Fig. 132: Baccarat open concentric. Note arrow canes in outer ring.

Fig. 133: Clichy open concentric on color ground. Note central Clichy rose cane.

grounds very effectively in conjunction with the simple five-cane spacing scheme described above. French glass workers coming to work in the glasshouses in the U.S. probably influenced the American carpet ground. (See Fig. 27, No. 2) The most sought after, and undoubtedly the most striking, spaced millefiori are the Clichy moss-green carpet grounds. The prize possessions of a few advanced collectors, these weights feature a ground of many small green canes contrasting jubilantly with the colorful spaced florets.

OPEN CONCENTRICS: These are concentric paperweights where space is left between the circles of canes; the background design is consequently more important. Usually there are no more than three circles of millefiori in an open concentric paperweight.

Clichy: (Figs. 131, 133) This was a common spacing scheme used by Clichy, often enhanced by the presence of a number of Clichy rose canes. Probably the largest paperweight made by Clichy was an open concentric with a diameter of 4⅝″ containing 64 Clichy roses. Many open concentrics were placed on lace grounds, but examples are extant on clear and various color grounds as well.

Baccarat: Open concentric Baccarat weights (Fig. 132, also see Fig. 121, No. 6) often include such characteristic rods as arrowhead, star and stardust canes in alternating colors; most colors are muted, making generous use of white, red, green and blue. In most examples the florets are set on a clear crystal ground. One example, however, features large complex canes in open concentric circles resting on an upset muslin ground. Butterfly silhouettes enhance this special weight.

NEGC: The open concentrics of the New England Glass Company most often contain two rows of concentric millefiori, and usually feature a peculiar type of latticinio backdrop. This was formed when the glass blowers allowed the ends of the collapsed latticinio cylinder to remain in the design — the ends of the cylinder then took the form of two tails, one tapering from the latticinio cushion downwards toward the base of the weight and the other extending upwards to support the central cane or floret around which the outer rings of millefiori are arranged. Occasionally one comes across a layer of "flashing," often purple-red or light green, placed between latticinio layers. Some NEGC open concentrics were faceted. Often each ring of the typical New England concentric is composed of identical canes; the colors of various rings are usually contrasted.

CLOSE CONCENTRICS: Concentric millefiori patterns are said to be "close" when there are so many circles of canes that the space between them is negligible. The regularity of the circles distinguishes this type of weight from the close pack millefiori design already discussed. In The Encyclopedia of Glass Paperweights, Paul Hollister says the design looks like a "set of false teeth" in some uninspired British pieces, and for other examples he likens close concentrics to a "formal garden." We are quick to acknowledge that in close concentrics, as at Versailles, gradation in size and cautious use of contrasting colors are crucial to a pleasing design.

Clichy: (Fig. 139) Clichy close concentrics are usually edged by an outer row of flat glass rods or staves; these rods — of a single, or more interestingly, of alternating colors — are pulled down to meet in the center of the base to form a "basket" for the weight's other contents. Pedestal or piedouche weights display staves which are pulled down through the foot. (Fig. 134) Clichy is particularly famous for these magnificent pieces.

St. Louis: The close concentric motif was the most prevalent of St. Louis spacing designs. Most of the cane arrangements thus classified contain nine or ten concentric circles and feature a "basket" of pulled-down canes. Large "SL" or small "SL 1848" canes sometimes appear in one of the outer rows (See Fig. 20, No. 5, Fig. 21, No. 3). A number of weights are also extant with the signature and date cane inserted upside down, resulting in a mirror image of the cane. (Refer to Dates and Signatures, page 36.) Central silhouette canes of animals or dancing figures in close concentrics are rarer. (Fig. 135)

Bacchus: This spacing scheme was a Bacchus favorite, and many examples were executed with a brashness perhaps indicative of the innovative tide of glass manufacture in post-glass-tax England. The rows of millefiori canes, forming a cushion, appear to be quite close to the top of the weight's dome and sometimes seem to be bursting forth like a frozen fireworks pinwheel. Pastel hues are characteristic of this factory.

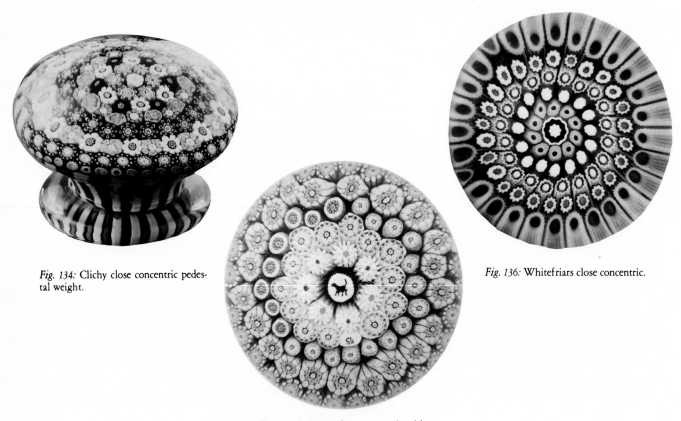

Fig. 134: Clichy close concentric pedestal weight.

Fig. 136: Whitefriars close concentric.

Fig. 135: St. Louis close concentric with signature cane and dog silhouette.

Whitefriars: (Figs. 136, 137) It is among these weights (See also Fig. 121, No. 8), the bulk of Whitefriars paperweight production, that one finds the "false teeth" appearance as noted by Hollister. They can be distinguished from Bacchus close concentrics by their smaller general cane size.

NEGC: (See Fig. 121, No. 3) Examples of close concentric weights from this factory are rare. They tend to be smallish; irregularly chopped-off cane bottoms are another characteristic. Usually they contain no ground, but are simply set in clear glass.

Whether woven to celebrate love, victory, or merely beauty, the millefiori garlands contained in certain patterned spacing schemes are among the most graceful and delicate ornaments found in paperweights.

CIRCULAR GARLANDS: These are millefiori chains set in either small ringlets or semi-circles.

Baccarat: (Fig. 138) These attractive circular garlands by Baccarat contain a central ring of canes surrounded by six additional ringlets, each centered on its own complex floret. This type of arrangement often features typical geometric canes such as arrow or stardust millefiori.

Fig. 137, Whitefriars close concentric mushroom double overlay.

Fig. 138, Baccarat circular garland.

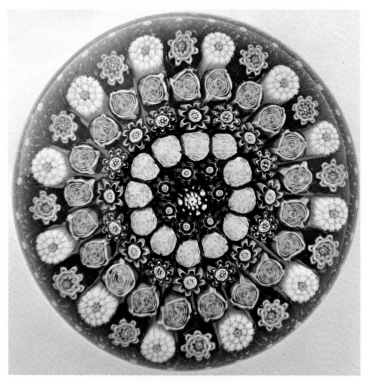

Fig. 139: Clichy close concentric millefiori.

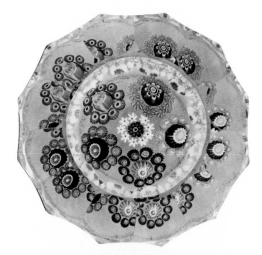

Fig. 141: Clichy faceted circular garland.

Fig. 142: Baccarat trefoil garland.

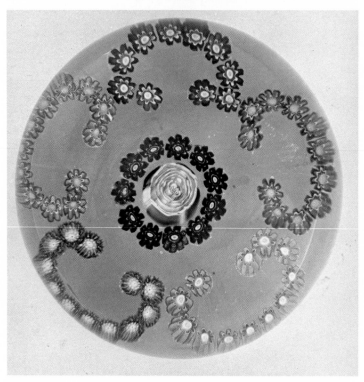

Fig. 140: Clichy C-scroll garlands.

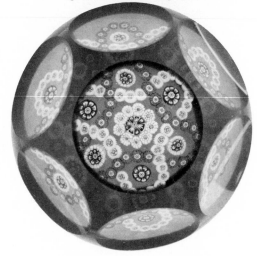

Fig. 143: Baccarat flash overlay with interlacing trefoil garlands.

Fig. 146: Clichy looped garland on lacy ground.

Fig. 144: Clichy star garlands.

Fig. 147: Clichy garlands on color ground.

Fig. 145: Clichy interlacing garlands.

Fig. 148: St. Louis looped garland.

Clichy: (Fig. 141) Like Baccarat, Clichy produced a design containing six circlets; the Clichy garland often surrounds a central Clichy rose. These circlets or ringlets are set on lacy, color or clear grounds. Identifiable Clichy florets such as the edelweiss and moss-green canes are commonly employed in this design.

A modified version of the circular garland is found in Clichy "C-scroll" paperweights (Fig. 140). A "C-scroll" is a semi-circular garland forming a "C" — a unique method of signing weights occasionally used by the Clichy factory. In some weights, with clear, lacy, or colored grounds, a series of five or six of these semi-circular garlands surround a central ring of canes, the whole being centered on a complex floret.

LOOPED GARLANDS: Looped garlands are those in which contiguous chains of millefiori canes form various undulating and/or interlacing designs. Trefoils (three loops), quatrefoils (four loops), and "star" (loops in a star shape) motifs fall in this category. Baccarat and Clichy, and to a much lesser extent St. Louis, marketed these designs.

Baccarat: The majority of these weights appear on clear grounds, although some featuring lace or color backdrops do exist. One Baccarat example shows a red, white, and blue color scheme incorporated in two interlacing trefoil garlands (Fig. 142); the weight rests on a pedestal with a blue-and-white filigree twist flange around the base. The looped garland motif was also included in Baccarat overlay paperweights, quite often featuring silhouette canes (Fig. 143).

Clichy: Clichy looped garlands occur mostly on colored or lacy cushions (Fig. 146); only a few are wrapped in clear glass (See Fig. 23, Nos. 1, 7). Opaque colored grounds used include salmon, apple green, amethyst, royal blue, turquoise (Fig. 147); some of the transparent color grounds common in looped garlands from this factory are cranberry, green, blue, and red.

The star garland arrangements (Fig. 144), a series of concentric star-shaped chains of millefiori canes, was also favored by Clichy (See Fig. 23, No. 5).

St. Louis: Looped garlands from this factory are extremely rare (Fig. 148). Usually a six-looped or diamond-shaped cluster of chains is centered on a large floret; this spacing scheme always appears on a colored ground in St. Louis paperweights.

PANEL PAPERWEIGHTS: The spacing schemes of most traditionally-shaped glass paperweights follow circular patterns. "Panel" paperweights produced by all three French factories represent a standard departure, whereby the weight is visually divided into "pie piece" sections by rods, rows of canes, or spacing between clusters. Often the canes between the divisions are referred to as "panels" and the separating elements, when present, are termed "spokes." Sometimes a panel motif is placed on a color ground; sometimes it rests on a cushion carpeted with complimentary millefiori canes.

St. Louis: (See Fig. 20, No. 4) St. Louis panel weights used jasper grounds of alternating colors (often red, green, blue, and white), centering the spokes around a turban swirl center or a silhouette cane. These weights contain an unusual torsade which is visible only from the side.

Baccarat: (Fig. 150) Baccarat weights of this type are often referred to as "carpets of clusters." Actually, the arrangement is a variation on the panel theme: the panels are made of millefiori, the dividing spokes are comprised by contrasting millefiori, and the background is a carpet ground of millefiori.

Clichy: Clichy panel weights often contain roses. (Fig. 149) One example, in fact, is said to have six panels, each panel composed entirely of these characteristic millefiori blooms. Nearly all of these stunning weights are set in color grounds. (See Fig. 121, No. 5).

Fig. 149: Detail of Clichy panel weight.

Special Millefiori Paperweight Types

MUSHROOMS: Resembling the edible fungus in shape, these popular paperweights usually employ a close pack, close concentric, or carpet ground motif within a "tuft" of millefiori canes pulled out to form a stem, then flaring again at the base. Most examples include a torsade encircling this stem. An air ring is frequently present above and below the torsade.

Clichy: (Figs. 152, 153) Mushrooms by Clichy usually occur in overlay paperweights, though a few stragglers appear in non-overlay versions. The canes comprising the tuft usually conform to a close pack or close concentric spacing pattern; the outer row of the pattern is often composed of striped staves (See Fig. 24, No. 3). No torsades were placed about Clichy mushrooms, but the bases were fancifully cut. Non-overlay mushroom weights are found with faceting similar to that used on the overlay version.

St. Louis: (Fig. 154) These mushroom weights most often utilize a close concentric spacing scheme and feature torsades in various colors (blue most frequently; also red, pink, and yellow). It should be remembered that the spiral within the torsade leans to the right when viewed from the side. Date and/or signature canes are sometimes present. A few St. Louis mushrooms have amber flash bottoms (Fig. 151). The majority, however, are clear with star-cut bases. No St. Louis antique mushroom overlays are known.

Baccarat: Baccarat mushrooms are most frequently found with a close pack millefiori tuft (Fig. 155), but come in concentric millefiori tufts as well. One lovely pattern is the white carpet ground mushroom commonly referred to as the "bouquet de marriage"; it features a tuft composed entirely of identical white stardust canes. Showy double overlay mushroom weights were also made at Baccarat and are considered rare.

Torsades are the frequent companions of Baccarat mushrooms and, as in the case of St. Louis mushrooms, blue is usually the color. However, red, pink, and white torsades are also found. Baccarat mushrooms are easily distinguished from their St. Louis counterparts by the direction of the spiral within the torsade. When viewed from the side Baccarat spirals lean to the left. No dated Baccarat mushrooms are recorded, although occasionally a silhouette cane may be included in the motif.

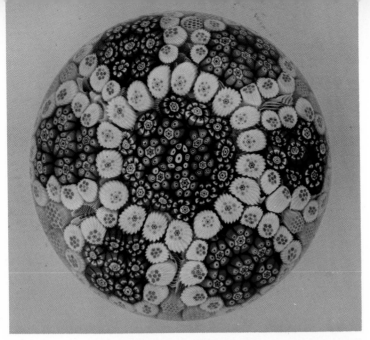

Fig. 150: Baccarat panel weight on honeycomb carpet ground.

Fig. 151: St. Louis amber flash mushroom.

Fig. 153: Clichy double overlay mushroom.

Fig. 154: St. Louis mushroom, viewed from top.

Fig. 152: Clichy mushroom double overlay, viewed from top.

Fig. 157: St. Louis marbrie weight.

Fig. 155: Baccarat mushroom. (Note direction of torsade)

Fig. 156: NEGC mushroom nosegay, side view.

Fig. 158: NEGC mushroom nosegay, top view.

NEGC: (Figs. 156, 158) The few mushroom weights produced in this Cambridge factory are usually quite special: they include overlays with fancy faceting and a unique design in which a nosegay floats in the center of a hollow-core mushroom form.

CROWN WEIGHTS

These stylized designs consist of a series of parallel, colored twists and filigree radiating from a central cane at the top of the weight's dome and running down the sides to the bottom center of the weight. Central florets and alternating twists vary in color and size; as many as 30 strands have been used to form the ribs of the "crown." The center of a crown weight is hollow; the air pocket occasionally comes through the base of the weight.

St. Louis: (See Fig. 121, No. 2) Crown weights were a St. Louis invention and are practically unique to this factory.

NEGC: (See Fig. 27, No. 3) The crown motif was imitated in America by the New England Glass Company, but these renderings are not as genteel: the surrounding glass is usually thicker and there are fewer ribs.

MARBRIE PAPERWEIGHTS: (Fig. 157) Another speciality of St. Louis was the "marbled" paperweight: a hollow globe of white glass was decorated with a central floret and loopings of brightly colored glass, often placed in a looped pattern around the sides. This type of paperweight was not manufactured in large quantities.

SWIRL PAPERWEIGHTS: (See Figs. 24, Nos. 2 and 4, also Fig. 23, No. 6) Clichy made a "swirl paperweight" with a central floret as the starting point for a pinwheel arrangement of opaque tubes. Some examples of this motif utilize two or three alternating colors; the most sought after swirl weights are those with a Clichy rose as the central floret.

Representational Paperweights — Floral

The subjects of these weights are all representational, in that they draw their inispiration from flowers, fruits, and a variety of animal life.

The accurate identification of an antique paperweight of this type is frequently quite difficult. The quest is aided immensely if millefiori canes are present — as part of a flower, as a garland surrounding a central motif, or below the main motif. The following descriptions of the ways in which various common representational motifs were handled by different factories of the Classical Period are designed to aid the collector in the identification of representational paperweights.

Dating: One type of millefiori cane which does not exist in *genuinely* antique floral paperweights is a date or signature cane.

Petal and Leaf Construction: Much has been written about the leaf structure and colors in floral paperweights, but there are no hard and fast rules that can be used for identification purposes. Some examples: St. Louis leaves are usually deeply serrated; but some

Baccarat, Clichy, and American flowers have similar leaves. Studying a number of floral weights will help the collector develop an intuition for leaf shape and color, but intuitional attributions are seldom terribly impressive to fellow collectors or prospective purchasers of a paperweight.

The color and structure of floral motifs can, however, be a dead give-away for inexpensive modern copies of antique weights. Many of these are of Chinese origin (See Fig. 260 Modern Chinese) and are characterized by the obvious use of orange, bright yellow, and bright green. Muranese imitations may often be distinguished from their models by the thickness of the flower petals and the coarseness of the latticinio grounds employed (Fig. 159). The novice collector should familiarize him- or herself with such paperweights by looking at the pieces sold in local gift shops.

Fig. 159: Modern Italian flower bouquet on coarse latticinio ground.

PANSY PAPERWEIGHTS

Baccarat: The most numerous of all paperweight flowers is the pansy, and of all the myriad pansy paperweights, the vast majority were manufactured at Baccarat. Approximately one quarter of the floral weights produced by Baccarat were of this species. There are three types of Baccarat pansies, which differ from one another in the construction of their lower petals, the formation of the other parts of the flower being largely standardized. The basic pansy consists of two large upper petals and three lower petals fixed on a stem with numerous green leaves; a bi-colored bud is also often present. The top petals have a velvety appearance obtained by using transparent purple glass over opaque white glass.

The most realistic pansy variation has three lower petals which are shallow opaque white cups filled with translucent yellow glass. On each of these lower petals three dark stripes radiate from the center of the flower; a large purple dot rests on the outer edge of the petal, and above the juncture of all five petals is a millefiori cane, usually a red or green whorl surrounded by white star rods or a honeycomb cane (Fig. 162). Although pansies of this variety were produced as late as the twentieth century and occasionally contain spurious date canes, they are easily distinguished from the genuine articles by the muddy yellow of their petals.

The second type of Baccarat pansy is similar in construction to the first except for the fact that there are no stripes or dots on the petals (Fig. 161). Instead, the petals are outlined in dark purple. There are a few examples of this type in which the blossom is mounted on a long curved stem with a bud.

A third pansy type features three cogwheel or arrow canes as the lower petals (Fig. 163). These canes were simply the ordinary millefiori canes used in other types of Baccarat paperweights, but they were not pulled out as far and had larger diameters. The petals may show dark arrows against a light ground or the reverse.

All three types of pansies may be found surrounded by a circle of canes and/or set on a bed of lace; latticinio or color grounds, however, are not known. A type one Baccarat pansy on a clear ground with star-cut base is one of the least expensive floral antique paperweights obtainable; it is, therefore, highly recommended as a good starting point for the accumulation of a paperweight flower garden.

The American equivalent of the Baccarat pansy has been dubbed the "weedflower" (Fig. 160). Produced by Sandwich on clear, latticinio, and spatter grounds, this motif enjoyed great popularity and was manufactured in quantities second only to the ubiquitous Sandwich poinsettias. The two plain top petals and two striped bottom petals of the "weedflower" were manufactured in a variety of colors and many different complex canes were used to represent stamen; consequently, no two of these wayward blooms seems to have been put together in exactly the same way.

Other Factories: Pansies were not a specialty of either the St. Louis or Clichy factories. Each, however, produced their own stylized varieties, the Clichy specimen resembling

Fig. 160: Sandwich pansy or "Weed-flower."

Fig. 162: Baccarat pansy.

Fig. 161: Baccarat pansy.

Fig. 163: Baccarat pansy with serrated lower petals.

the charming "Johnny Jump Ups." These pieces are quite rare but do not achieve the realism set by Baccarat (See Fig. 24, No. 1).

NOSEGAYS: Sometimes termed "posies" or, in reference to their two-dimensional nature, "flat bouquets," nosegays are representations of an arrangement of three to five flowers on four or more green leaves. The flowers and leaves are represented by millefiori canes and the leaf canes are pulled into a stem. A considerable number of variations were wrought from this basic design. In its simplest form the nosegay is set in clear crystal. Embellished, it appears with an encircling ring of canes, with simple to complex faceting, and on an upset muslin ground or with amber flashing. Strawberry-diamond cutting was sometimes done on the base. More than one nosegay occasionally appears in a single magnum weight.

St. Louis: (See Fig. 22, Nos. 5, 6) Most nosegay paperweights were manufactured by St. Louis; they established the prototype described above and had great influence on the manufacture of floral paperweights in the United States (See "NEGC Nosegays" below). One unusual St. Louis variation features a circle of nosegays in a magnum weight. There are no known Baccarat nosegays.

Clichy: Clichy produced nosegays in very limited numbers utilizing clear or lacy grounds. Most desirable, of course, are those featuring the Clichy rose as one of the flower canes (Fig. 164).

NEGC: (Fig. 165) Perhaps it was Nicholas Lutz who fostered the idea of producing nosegay paperweights at the New England Glass Company; at any rate, those made at NEGC bear a remarkable resemblance to those manufactured in Lutz' home town of St. Louis. Made from three different complex canes resting on four leaves, they are rather mechanistic in construction, with two horizontally aligned leaves facing left and right and two almost vertical leaves pointing away from the stem. This design is found on clear, latticinio, and sometimes colored grounds; several types ·of faceting, including quatrefoil cuts on top and vertical flutes on sides of paperweights, were used. One unusual variation of the NEGC nosegay, where the bouquet floats inside a mushroom-like hollow tuft of millefiori canes (See Fig. 156) has already been mentioned (refer to "Mushrooms," page 65); in another singular piece, an NEGC artisan included a pear with a nosegay bouquet.

PRIMROSE PAPERWEIGHTS: All primrose-type flower motifs were characterized by rounded or heart-shaped petals; some were circled by millefiori garlands; some appeared with one or more color-matched buds, against the backdrop of a star-cut base, or in various faceted paperweights.

Baccarat: Two types of petals were used in the unique Baccarat floral paperweights known as "primroses." The first type was made from five cup-shaped petals. Inserts of contrasting colors were placed in the petals, allowing only the ruffled edge of the lower cup to show (See Fig. 19, No. 5). The junction of the petals was covered with a mille-

Fig. 164: Clichy nosegay.

Fig. 166: Baccarat clematis with two buds.

Fig. 165: NEGC nosegay on latticinio.

fiori cane, usually of the stardust variety. Green leaves appeared behind the flower head and on the stem; occasionally a bud was added.

The second type of primrose has a flatter appearance consisting of six petals of either red or blue. A white band decorates the middle of each petal (See Fig. 171, No. 7).

Another exclusively Baccarat flower of the primrose type is called the wallflower (Fig. 167). These rare blossoms usually have five white petals edged in a color and may be accompanied by a matching bud. An arrow cane or honeycomb cane generally serves as the stamen cluster.

St. Louis: Similar to the Baccarat primrose-type flowers in petal shape, the St. Louis pelargonium or geranium has five heart-shaped petals, each bearing two short black stripes, manufactured in pink or red tones. This was a popular element in bouquet paperweights (See Fig. 172, No. 7).

CLEMATIS PAPERWEIGHTS: Flowers comprised of one or two layers of *pointed* veined petals are grouped together in the "clematis" category: a one-layer clematis is called a "single clematis" and two layer blooms are termed "double."

Baccarat: Baccarat for the most part produced a double clematis, with each layer containing six petals. A single clematis was also made, but it usually occurs in a composition of two or more flowers (See Fig. 171, No. 4).

One type of Baccarat clematis is characterized by two buds accompanying the main bloom, growing at right angles to the flower stalk. The buds are supported by two auxiliary stems which twist about the central stalk below the flower (Fig. 166). A closely related flower shows the bloom with more conventional foliage (See Fig. 171, No. 2).

Fig. 167: Baccarat wallflower.

A twisting arrangement of bud-bearing stems is also found in some weights containing no fully-developed flowers. These are known as "clematis-bud" paperweights (Fig. 168, also see Fig. 172, No. 3). The buds and the clematis flower just described occur in pink, white, yellow and aqua. Occasionally two colors of buds are used in the same weight.

Another beautiful Baccarat clematis has elongated pointed petals in which an unusual veining is achieved by alternating thin strips of clear and colored glass (Fig. 169); a rare variation on the clematis theme is the "wheatflower." This variety is wrought in yellow or white glass and shows two or three small dots on each petal. These are quite attractive and command high prices.

In general, Baccarat clematis flowers are most often found with a honeycomb or star-dust center, a clear ground and a star-cut base.

St. Louis: St. Louis also made many variations of the clematis. Often it appears with a yellow, red, or white "matchhead" or dot center (Figs. 170, 176, also see Fig. 172, No. 2), although the characteristic 14-cog millefiori was also used to represent stamens. Blossoms of blue, pink, white or a rare striped variety of blossoms were generally placed on clear, jasper, or latticinio grounds. Extremely rare exceptions feature colored or aventurine backdrops.

American Variations: The American equivalent of the clematis-type flower is the poinsettia, produced in great quantities by both Sandwich and the New England Glass Company. High-domed examples of this species, usually having a deep concave bottom, are attributed to NEGC; those with flatter profiles, sometimes containing the Lutz interpretation of the Clichy rose as a central stamen, are accredited to Sandwich

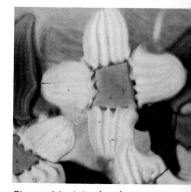

Fig. 170: Match head or dot centers used in some St. Louis flower weights.

Fig. 168: Baccarat clematis-bud weight.

Fig. 169: Baccarat clematis and bud.

Fig. 171: **A PAPERWEIGHT FLOWER GARDEN.** *Top row, No. 1,* Baccarat buttercup; *No. 2,* Baccarat white double clematis. *Middle row, No. 3,* Baccarat anemone or primrose; *No. 4,* Baccarat two flower bouquet featuring a single clematis and double clematis; *No. 5,* Sandwich poinsettia. *Bottom row, No. 6,* A faceted Baccarat variegated pom-pom within a circle of canes; *No. 7,* Baccarat primrose; *No. 8,* Baccarat buttercup with bud.

Fig. 172: **A PAPERWEIGHT FLOWER GARDEN.** *Clockwise from top,* No. 1, St. Louis fuchsia on latticinio ground; *No. 2,* St. Louis double clematis on latticinio; *No. 3,* Baccarat clematis-bud weight; *No. 4,* Sandwich poinsettia on jasper ground; *No. 5,* Baccarat pansy; *No. 6,* Sandwich cross flower on jasper ground. *Center, No. 7,* St. Louis mixed bouquet centering on a pelargonium or geranium.

(See Fig. 171, No. 5 and Fig. 172, No. 4). American poinsettias appear on clear, jasper, and latticinio grounds.

Other variations of the clematis, generally attributed to Sandwich, are a Baccarat-style "wheatflower," a striped poinsettia flower, and a double clematis with upright petal, closely resembling a rose (Fig. 173).

DAHLIA: The dahlia paperweight floral motif can be looked upon as a clematis carried to its logical extreme. Here there are as many as five layers of petals — 40 or more individual petals — in the blossom. Needless to say, perfect or near-perfect examples of this design are quite hard to find.

St. Louis: The dahlia was produced most successfully by St. Louis. In these floral paperweights the five overlapping rings of petals usually radiate from a single cane; a few green leaves and short stem are barely visible at the edge of the flower (Fig. 178).

Other Factories: Clichy and Baccarat produced dahlias only to a very limited extent. In the United States, the Mt. Washington Glass Works created a spectacular magnum dahlia.

POM-POM PAPERWEIGHTS: The "pom-pom" or "camomile" is interpreted in paperweights as a three-dimensional, multi-celled flower, composed of many tiny pockets or cells around a cane center. Most pom-poms are virtuoso demonstrations of the seemingly miraculous level of technical ability attained by nineteenth-century glassworkers.

St. Louis: Compared with its Baccarat counterpart, the pom-pom manufactured by St. Louis is more hemispherical in shape and sometimes has a feathery or wispy appearance at the outer ends of the flower cells (Fig. 174). Invariably two leaves are set behind the bloom, a good rule for identification. A bud and a stem bearing green leaves usually compliment the flower. White or pink blossoms set on a white or pink swirling latticinio ground were employed in other variations. Rare examples show shades of red latticinio alternating with white, dramatically showing off a delicate white bloom.

Fig. 173: American double clematis, resembling rose.

Baccarat: The Baccarat pom-pom is flatter on top than the St. Louis version of this motif, and its cells are quite precise and sharp (Fig. 175). Four or more leaves, and occasionally a bud, appear from behind the flower head; a stalk with two leaves supports the flower. White, yellow, red, blue/white (See Fig. 171, No. 6), and the rare copper-colored blossoms were made with matching or contrasting buds. Usually set on a clear ground, many pom-pom paperweights have encircling rings of millefiori canes and feature a variety of faceting designs. These weights are scarcer than those of St. Louis.

NEGC: The New England Glass Company also created a successful pom-pom; however, only a few good examples are extant.

UPRIGHT BOUQUET PAPERWEIGHTS: As the term suggests, these are weights in which a three-dimensional bouquet of clematis and simple cane flowers is featured, placed upright in the dome with the stem pulled down to the base. As in mushroom weights, a filigree torsade circling the base of this pulled stem is often used to emphasize the "depth" effect.

Baccarat: Relatively few upright bouquets were made by Baccarat. Identification is usually based on the type of millefiori used in the flowers or by the direction of the spiral in the encircling filigree torsade: if the spiral leans to the left when viewed from the side it's a Baccarat (Fig. 180).

St. Louis: St. Louis used the upright bouquet motif much like Baccarat. However, they also utilized it in a small number of overlay paperweights (Fig. 181), and for the extremely rare encased overlays (where an ordinary overlay was reheated and encased in clear crystal). The spiral torsades in these weights lean to the right when viewed from the side. Upright bouquets were also used by this factory to adorn decanter stoppers, bowl tops, and other objects (Fig. 179).

NEGC: Some of the best-crafted antique American paperweights are the upright bouquets manufactured by the New England Glass Company. Some were magnum-sized with the floral motif resting on a latticinio ground; others were fashioned into elaborately faceted single and double overlays.

Fig. 174: (left), St. Louis pom-pom or camomile; *Fig. 175:* Baccarat pom-pom or camomile.

Fig. 177: St. Louis clematis.

Fig. 176: St. Louis flower bouquet with "match head" centers.

Fig. 178: St. Louis dahlia.

Fig. 179: St. Louis water set. Two decanters, sugar bowl, glass. All stoppers contain upright bouquets.

Fig. 180: Baccarat upright bouquet.

Fig. 181: St. Louis upright bouquet.

81

ROSE PAPERWEIGHTS

Baccarat: (See Fig. 188) Baccarat introduced a well-executed thousand-petalled rose, sometimes appearing with a bud. A number of leaves frame the blossom and also adorn the stem. Colors of flower and bud vary from pink to ruby; bases are generally clear and star-cut.

Clichy: In the beautiful and rare Clichy rose weight, the familiar Clichy rose cane is used for the entire blossom. Slightly larger than when it appears in a millefiori weight, the cane in this instance is tilted a bit, and supported by a stem with leaves and a bud.

Mt. Washington: (See frontispiece) Like all paperweights crafted at Mt. Washington, the rose weights are quite large. This Yankee species features a ruffled petal motif and an occasional gold stone center. The blossom is set on a stalk which may also bear a single bud or two buds in opposition. Occasionally a hand is shown holding the flowers, or a butterfly is added to the composition.

ONE-FACTORY FLOWERS: These are floral paperweight types made by only one factory, so identification is greatly simplified.

Baccarat: The "bellflower" motif (Fig. 185), a trio of hanging flowers on stems, with a bud and many leaves, was made only by Baccarat. These rare weights have appreciated considerably in recent years. Another unique Baccarat creation was a three-dimensional "buttercup" paperweight: these blooms consist of an outer circle of six deeply-cupped petals under an inner ring of five small (cupped) petals centered on a millefiori cane. Many color combinations were used for this two-tiered petal system. Buttercups (Figs. 182, 186) were produced in all sizes, including a popular miniature variety.

St. Louis: Until the advent of the Whittemore fuchsia (See Fig. 275) in recent years, St. Louis was the only factory to create one of these semi-tropical blooms in glass. Their version (See Fig. 172, No. 1), set on a russet-colored stem and grouped with a berry, one or more buds, and four leaves, rests on a clear or latticinio ground. Variations are also found with two flowers on the stem.

Fig. 182: Baccarat buttercup.

Clichy: Clichy produced a "convolvulus" or "morning glory" floral paperweight which is one of the rarest of all single-blossom weights. Resting on either a clear or a latticinio ground, the trumpet-like flower is seen in combinations of white, yellow, pink, and blue.

Clichy also fashioned a unique variety of clematis and other round-petaled flowers. In constructing the petals they experimented with canes and simple white lobes, as well as the veined pointed shapes already employed by other factories.

The "lily-of-the-valley" is perhaps Clichy's most unique floral motif: it features an arrangement of many white blooms and three green leaves, poised on a single stem. The motif is set on a brilliant red ground. This paperweight holds the price record for an auction sale: $22,000.

FLORAL BOUQUET PAPERWEIGHTS: All the French factories (Figs. 187, 188, 189, 190, 191), and the Mt. Washington Glass Works in Massachusetts, produced a variety of paperweights containing more than one lampworked flower (See frontispiece). Almost all combinations of flowers were tried, some more successfully than others. These bouquet weights are generally over 3″ in diameter. Sometimes the flowers were spaced to form a symmetrical pattern, with four flowers surrounding a central blossom. Good examples of French bouquet paperweights are quite rare and command top prices.

The Incredible Mt. Washington Floral Plaque: (Fig. 184) Aesthetically and technically, one of the most extraordinary paperweights ever produced is the Mt. Washington floral plaque. This truly distinctive creation contains a bouquet of up to 13 small dahlia-like flowers and buds, their green stems gracefully tied together with a ribbon. The usual dimensions of this unusual piece, of which only four examples are extant, are approximately 5″ x 3½″ x 1″. The edges are beveled and the bottoms are diamond cut, frosted, or clear.

Fig. 183: St. Louis two-flower bouquet.

Fig. 184: Mt. Washington plaque.

Fig. 185: Baccarat bellflower.

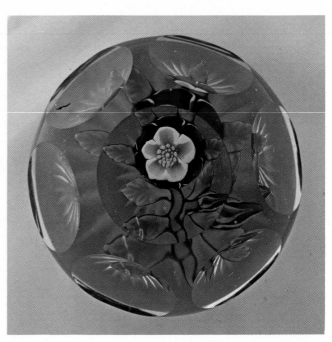

Fig. 186: Baccarat buttercup.

84

Fig. 187: Baccarat floral bouquet.

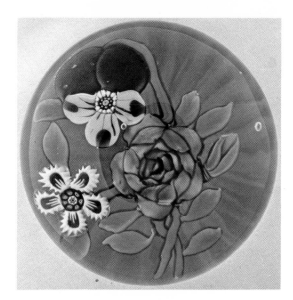

Fig. 188: Baccarat bouquet with thousand petal rose.

Fig. 189: Clichy bouquet.

Fig. 190: St. Louis bouquet with pelargonium.

Fig. 191: Baccarat bouquet with central buttercup.

Representational Paperweights — Fruit

MIXED FRUIT PAPERWEIGHTS: Among the most colorful of all paperweights, and among the easiest to ascribe to a factory, is the mixed fruit paperweight. These were produced at St. Louis, Sandwich and the NEGC. Some of the American mixed fruit paperweights, unfortunately, look like the first attempt of an apprentice; others, although quite acceptable, are nevertheless inferior to their St. Louis counterparts. The French fruit seems more realistic and appealing and the St. Louis latticinio is more delicate and finely-shaped (Fig. 193).

St. Louis: The general configuration included three pears or apples and a number of cherries on a bed of serrated green leaves; below the fruit, a swirling latticinio ground was pulled down in the enter to form a basket (See Fig. 193, No. 3).

American Factories: Both Sandwich (See Fig. 193, No. 2) and the New England Glass Company produced a formalized fruit paperweight; attribution of a particular example to one factory or the other is difficult, however, because a similar pattern was used by both. Pears in shades of yellow to red are centered on a fifth pear and set on a bed of four leaves; four more leaves and several cherries are inserted in the remaining spaces. Latticinio grounds are most common, although clear grounds have been observed. Usually those that are high-domed and have deeply concave basal grinding are attributed to the NEGC, while those which are flatter in profile are assigned to Sandwich.

STRAWBERRY PAPERWEIGHTS

St. Louis: (See Fig. 193, No. 7) This factory joined a five-petaled white clematis-type flower on a long stem with a number of leaves and two large hanging strawberries — one ripe, the other green. The stylization is found most often on a swirling latticinio ground. These weights are rare, and examples with unbroken stems and perfect petals are harder still to acquire.

Baccarat: These are so incredibly realistic they seem fresh-plucked from a summer field; Baccarat constructed them from many colored canes which were fused and then rounded to shape. The characteristic Baccarat rendition features two or three large berries in various stages of ripeness with leaves and interconnecting stems. Baccarat strawberry paperweights are rare.

Mt. Washington: These magnum pieces contain five large berries on leafy beds, placed at random among four small, upright, white clematis-type flowers. Only a few examples are known.

OTHER TYPES OF FRUIT PAPERWEIGHTS: Although the mixed fruit and strawberry motifs account for a majority of antique representational fruit paperweights, other types were manufactured. These are best listed by factory.

St. Louis: St. Louis gathered two or more cherries (See Fig. 193, No. 5), or clusters of mulberries or grapes, into motifs similar to those found in their unique fuchsia paperweights (see "One Factory Flowers." page 82): the fruit hangs from an orange-brown stem set with two or more leaves. Many complex faceting patterns were used in conjunction with such weights, and some of the bases are also cut; clear grounds predominate. Pears, apples, and apricots have been ascribed to St. Louis (and Baccarat), but very few examples are extant.

St. Louis also produced a very limited number of blown fruit weights similar to the more common examples by NEGC.

St. Louis was the only factory to make a vegetable paperweight (See Fig. 22, No. 4). This rare motif was comprised by six colored turnips, root tips meeting at the center of the weight, with a number of short green leaves, set on a latticinio ground.

Clichy: No fruit weights of any kind are definitely known to have been produced by Clichy.

Sandwich: The influence of St. Louis products on those of the Sandwich factory in Massachusetts — perhaps exerted through Nicholas Lutz — is again apparent in fruit paperweights. Those made at Sandwich feature pairs of cherries (See Fig. 193, Nos. 1 and 6), pears, or blue plums, hanging on an interconnecting stem system with an arrangement of two large and two small serrated leaves. These weights are generally very well executed.

NEGC: (See Fig. 193, No. 4) Realistically-shaped and colored pears, apples, and quinces of blown glass on clear glass cushions were a specialty of the New England Glass Company. They are three-dimensional and are not enclosed in crystal; therefore, they cannot be considered to be in the truly classical tradition. They glisten charmingly, though, and highlight any paperweight collection.

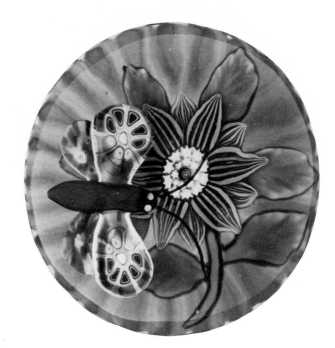

Fig. 192: Baccarat butterfly and flower.

Fig. 193: **ANTIQUE FRUIT WEIGHTS.** *Top, No. 1,* Sandwich cherry weight with two berries, leaves and stems. *Second row, No. 2,* Sandwich or N.E.G.C. mixed fruit on a latticinio basket; *No. 3,* St. Louis mixed fruit on a latticinio basket. *Center, No. 4,* N.E.G.C. blown pear on a round glass base. *Third row, No. 5,* St. Louis cherry weight with two berries hanging from an orange stem; *No. 6,* Sandwich pear weight with two fruits, stems and leaves. *Bottom, No. 7,* St. Louis strawberry on latticinio.

Fig. 194: American butterfly and fruit weight.

Representational Paperweights — Insects, Birds, and Reptiles

BUTTERFLY PAPERWEIGHTS

Baccarat: (Fig. 196) A very popular theme at Baccarat, the butterfly was constructed of two sets of very thin millefiori wings attached to a fine gauze body; eyes and antennae completed the motif, sometimes imperfectly. The insect is found on clear or lace ground, sometimes within a garland of canes or (less frequently) above any of the paperweight blossoms (See Fig. 192) detailed above. Most desirable among these weights is a combination of the butterfly and one of the rarer flowers. Perhaps the most unusual specimen shows the butterfly, with its wings closed, resting on a leafy branch. The Baccarat butterfly is basic to any advanced collection.

St. Louis: This factory also attempted butterfly weights; while technically correct, these are often aesthetically unsuccessful. The rare St. Louis examples on latticinio, for instance, sometimes suffer from an excess of bright color. For example, the butterfly might have a green-and-yellow-striped body, red-and-purple wings, and orange antennae. One creative worker placed a frog above a butterfly.

Clichy: Only one example of a Clichy butterfly has been found (Fig. 195): it has a plump, orange body with two sets of cane wings. The upper set of triangular wings is fashioned from pink rose canes with yellow centers, and the lower pair is made from whole pink Clichy roses with green staves. Eyes, rather crude antennae, and six minuscule legs are attached to the body.

NEGC: A single example of an American butterfly paperweight, probably produced by the New England Glass Company, is extant, although small butterflies occasionally complement Mt. Washington weights featuring floral motifs. The NEGC insect (Fig. 194) is red and blue with cane wings, resting on a diagonally striped branch. Two ripe yellow pears, two green leaves, and a latticinio basket complete the design, probably made by Nicholas Lutz.

BIRD PAPERWEIGHTS: Although the bird motif is not used extensively in antique glass paperweights, it is worth mentioning because a few fine examples have been reported.

St. Louis: A two-dimensional stylized bird with long legs, perched on a piece of greenery has been attributed to St. Louis. Also extant is a large weight with a red, yellow, and white bird inspecting a nest of three blue eggs; the entire motif is set within a framework of green branches.

Clichy: Clichy made a paperweight with a bird standing over a simple white flower above a bed of lace.

Baccarat: A design attributed to Baccarat features from one to three ducks or swans swimming in the bottom of a hollow space inside a large, faceted weight; the ground color is usually green.

Fig. 195: Clichy butterfly.

Fig. 196: Baccarat butterfly.

SNAKE PAPERWEIGHTS: A certain mystique surrounds the snake paperweights produced by Baccarat and St. Louis. They are highly sought after and, therefore, expensive.

Baccarat: These snakes were produced in red, pink, and green; they lie coiled on rocky, lacy or latticinio grounds. Sandy-grounded snake weights are always Baccarat weights (Fig. 199).

St. Louis: Snakes produced by St. Louis are found on lace, jasper, and various color grounds, but not on sand.

LIZARD OR SALAMANDER PAPERWEIGHTS: The precise motivation behind the creation of a multitude of salamander paperweights is not known, but the reptile does occupy an interesting position in glassmaking lore. In this regard, we quote Deming Jarvis who wrote, in *Reminiscences of Glass-Making* (1865):

> "Among these legends was that which ascribed to the furnace-fire the property of creating the monster called the Salamander. It was believed, too, that at certain times this wonderful being issued from his abode, and, as opportunity offered, carried back some victim to his fiery bed. The absence of workmen, who sometimes departed secretly for foreign lands, was always accounted for by the hypothesis that in some unguarded moment they had fallen prey to the Salamander."

Baccarat: The realistic reptiles by this factory are usually seen slithering around a floral arrangement of two or three white blossoms with yellow centers. Green foliage is also a frequent part of the composition. The typical ground is the sandy type used for Baccarat snakes.

St. Louis: (Figs. 197, 198) These rare weights are a peculiar mixture of a hollow, marbrie, or empty overlay paperweight and a three-dimensional salamander coiled on top. The reptile is sometimes covered or highlighted with gold; one rare specimen has a typical St. Louis millefiori cane embedded in its head. Copies of salamander weights have been made, but these are so poor in quality that even a novice collector should be able to distinguish them.

Fig. 197: St. Louis salamander.

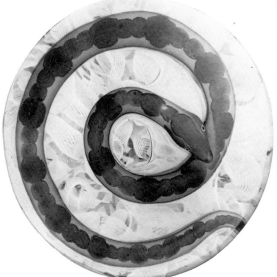

Fig. 199: Baccarat snake.

Fig. 198: St. Louis salamander.

Fig. 200: Top, No. 1, Framed plaque of reclining lady contemplating an oval portrait. *Left, No. 2*, Inkwell with sulphide in side and stopper. *Right, No. 3*, Apsley Pellat square shaped bottle with three sulphides, all signed "Patent London" on the reverse. *Bottom, No. 4*, Patch box with sulphide portrait of a child.

Fig. 201: Top row, No. 1, Bottle with bust of Napoleon; *No. 2*, Wine glass with sulphide of cardinal's emblem; *No. 3*, Plaque with original brass hanger, religious subject. *Bottom row, No. 4*, Vase with rare amber ground behind sulphide of Victoria; *No. 5*, Rectangular letter or paperweight with a military figure, heavy star-cut back; *No. 6*, Perfume or scent bottle with silver top, sulphide of a soldier.

Fig. 202: Sulphide of cardinal's seal on translucent red ground.

Fig. 203: Baccarat magnum sulphide of Queen Victoria.

Fig. 204: Tumblers with sulphides.

Sulphide Paperweights

The encasing of compatible ceramic objects in clear or colored crystal was a form of glass art that was mastered before the flourishing of millefiori technique in the 19th century. The Classical Period of sulphide production is therefore dated differently than the Classical Period for millefiori paperweight manufacture: it is approximately 1819 to 1865. A method of "Crystalo-Ceramie," or sulphide cameo incrustation in crystal, was patented by Apsley Pellat, an Englishman, in 1819 and the technique was subsequently developed in France by Pierre Honore Boudon de Saint-Amans.

Sulphide identification is rarely simple. It often involves historical research, since the sulphide motif frequently commemorated an event or honored a political or religious figure. Some cameo paperweights, however, are purely decorative. A wide variety of glass articles, including paperweights (Figs. 202, 203, 206), tumblers, decanters, bottles, perfumes, plaques, religious crosses, vases, plates, cups, steins, pitchers, jewelry, door knobs, seals, candlesticks, and pushplates, have all been used to house sulphides (Figs. 200, 201, 204, 205).

Only a very few sulphide paperweights bear identifying marks such as a signature, date, or subject name impressed or printed on the back of the cameo. Occasionally the inclusion of millefiori canes will aid in identification. Sometimes, too, a particular sulphide is the recognizable product of a particular factory. This is true in the case of a tumbler with an oval sulphide painted with a bouquet motif; this same element occurs in a positively-identified St. Louis carpet ground paperweight. Usually, though, sulphide identification and attribution is a matter of informed guesswork.

The lists below will help the collector identify the most common sulphide paperweights, factory by factory. For additional information, we heartily recommend a beautiful book on the subject, *Sulphides; The Art of Cameo Incrustation,* by Paul Jokelson.

BACCARAT: The most highly prized sulphides from Baccarat are a series of magnum paperweights with flat tops and diamond faceting, which feature four subjects: a hunter and dog, Joan of Arc (See Fig. 206), Queen Victoria (Fig. 203), and the Madonna. Grounds are transparent ruby, blue, or green.

Baccarat employed a variety of other motifs in sulphide paperweights, however. These include those with clear glass settings, some with color grounds, and some featuring one to three rings of millefiori canes. A few beautiful double overlay Baccarat sulphides are also extant.

Baccarat Sulphide Subjects

Benjamin Franklin	Louis Philip	St. Cecilia
Czar Nicholas I	Monseigneur Affre	St. Therese
Chateaubriand	Napoleon I	St. Vincent de Paul
Descent from the cross	Napoleon III	George Washington
Duke of Orleans	Pope Pius IX	Victoria and Albert

CLICHY: The sulphides produced by Clichy are nearly all set on opaque or translucent color grounds. Some examples include rings of millefiori canes, including Clichy roses, surrounding the cameo.

Clichy Sulphide Subjects

Alfred de Musset	Henry IV	Princess Eugenie
Cardinals' Emblems	Holy Family	St. Alesis
Charles X	Joan of Arc	St. Andrew
Chateaubriand	Louis Philip	St. Elizabeth
Comte de Chambord	Margaret Valois	St. Mary Magdalene
Czar Nicholas I	Marie Antoinette	St. Palmire
Exhibition Building, London, 1851	Napoleon I (in profile and full view)	St. Rene
Emperor Maximillian of Austria	Napoleon III	St. Vincent de Paul
Frederick VII of Denmark	Oscar I of Sweden	Victoria
General Taylor	Pope Pius IX	Virgin and Child

ST. LOUIS: St. Louis' sulphide production was more limited than that of Clichy or Baccarat. Most cameo pieces include a ring of millefiori around the sulphide; rarer examples include a spiral torsade surrounding the cameo, and a laurel wreath beneath the subject. One uncommon millefiori panel weight contains a sulphide in the center.

Fig. 205: Plates with allegorical sulphides.

A three-dimensional sulphide fish swimming over a jasper ground is also unique to St. Louis; a variation of this design includes a ring of characteristic St. Louis arrow canes on the perimeter of the ground.

St. Louis Sulphide Subjects

Bouquet (painted on a circular disc)	Josephine	Prince Albert
	Lamartine	Fish (upright)
Czar Nicholas I	Napoleon III	St. Clair
Descent from the cross	Pope Pius	Virgin Mary

BRITISH FACTORIES: Common subjects are listed below.

British Sulphide Subjects

Carolyn Bonaparte	William E. Gladstone	Prince Albert
Robert Burns	Greek and Roman scenes	Queen Anne
Duke of Wellington	John Heriot	Victoria

PORTUGUESE: Sulphide objects including tumblers, stemmed glasses, and plates, are known to have been manufactured in Portugal by Fabrica Vista Alegre, a glassworks near the small town of Aveiro, between 1837 and 1846.

Portuguese Sulphide Subjects

Dom Pedro, Duke of Braganca	King John VI	Queen Maria II
	Louiz de Camoens (poet)	Duke of Palmela

Fig. 206: Baccarat Joan of Arc sulphide.

Bottleweights

These objects, manufactured by bottle factories from glass left over at day's end, can scarcely be compared with classic paperweights. In fact, the English have nicknamed them "dumps" and "door-stops," a reflection on their humble origins.

For many years all bottleweights, except those signed otherwise, were attributed to the glassworks at Nailsea. Paul Hollister, however, contended in 1969 in *The Encyclopedia of Glass Paperweights,* that the areas of origin were Castleford and Wakefield in Yorkshire.

Bottleweights vary profusely in size, shape, and verdant intensity. They may be classified into one of the following four categories:

Sulphide Bottleweights: (Figs. 207, 208) It seems as if an infinite variety of bottleweight sulphides was produced; one rarely sees two similar objects. Busts of famous persons, figures of animals, and mottoes on plaques are placed, sometimes haphazardly, in the green glass. Some weights contain representations of historical figures from as late as the early twentieth century.

Bubble Bottleweights: (Fig. 209) The bubble-type weights consist of a series of evenly-spaced teardrop-shaped bubbles which fill the entire weight. They are especially attractive when lighted from below.

Floral Bottleweights: Probably the most popular of the bottleweights are those containing "potted plants." In these weights a silvery pot holds a stem and one or more multi-petaled flowers. Some examples have a series of small flowers arising from the pot. The silvery appearance of the subject is created by an enormous number of closely-spaced minute bubbles forming the design.

Foil-Design Bottleweights: Metallic foil, occasionally colored dark blue or black, is a part of some bottleweight designs. The foil was used both to enhance traditional designs such as the flowerpot mentioned above and to create abstract designs.

Most bottleweights are unsigned, but a number have been found with the words "J. Kilner, Maker, Wakefield" or "J. Kilner and Son(s)" impressed on the bottom. The age of these weights can be determined by the wording of the signature. The Birmingham establishment was called "J. Kilner" between 1829 and 1832. Its name changed to "J. Kilner and Son(s)" between 1832 and 1844. After this, the name was Kilner Brothers. These examples can therefore be termed the earliest datable English paperweights.

Fig. 207: Castleford sulphide of lady's head; *Fig. 208:* Castleford lady with cornucopia; *Fig. 209:* Castleford bubble weight.

Fig. 207

Fig. 208

Fig. 209

Chapter IV

The Paperweight Renaissance — The Factories

The term "renaissance" means, of course, "rebirth." The artists and factories discussed in this chapter are those who are exploring new possibilities using a rich, and recently rediscovered, classical heritage *from the past.* Other talented, creative artists are experimenting in the more recent Tiffany tradition, but this is quite different from the classical techniques of millefiori, lampwork, and sulphides and is best left to Chapter VI.

It was inevitable that the interest in antique glass paperweights should result in at least a limited resumption of the manufacture of traditional quality weights. Just how this happened is described in detail below, in a series of vignettes on various factories. Contemporary glass artists are dealt with in Chapter V.

Baccarat

The French seemingly lost touch with the art of millefiori decoration almost as rapidly as they developed it. In a 1914 memorandum to the Baccarat management it was stated that no craftsman survived who knew how to make millefiori canes. No written instructions were extant. This may or may not be true: the story goes that an elderly worker named Dupont retained some knowledge. Weights attributed to him, sometimes containing spurious date canes, were sold in the Baccarat retail outlet in Paris. However, the puzzling "Dupont" weights are, if anything, a part of the 19th century millefiori tradition rather than harbingers of a renaissance.

The renewed interest in paperweight manufacture at Baccarat was sparked in 1951. The excavation of the old Baccarat church, destroyed in the Second World War, unearthed a very unusual paperweight which had been embedded in the cornerstone (See Fig. 59). This weight, a close packed millefiori magnum with an 1853 date cane, was recorded in the Baccarat factory records as having been made by Martin Kayser. Kayser was employed at Baccarat from 1827 until his death in 1860. The paperweight has since become known as the "church weight" and is on display at the Baccarat showrooms in Paris. Although this unique discovery caught the imagination of the inheritors of the millefiori tradition, it remained for Paul Jokelson, a collector and importer, to inspire serious thoughts of reviving the industry.

In 1953, at Jokelson's urging, Baccarat attempted to produce a sulphide paperweight. It was based on Dwight Eisenhower's presidential campaign medal. 153 of these weights were made, but they were commercially unsuccessful because of the poor likeness of the sulphide. The experiment had convinced the glassworkers at Baccarat, however, that it was indeed possible to encase a sulphide cameo in glass.

Mr. Jokelson persisted in his quest. Baccarat subsequently produced and issued a sulphide weight of Queen Elizabeth II and H.R.H. the Duke of Edinburgh for the Queen's coronation (1953). The overwhelming commercial success of this paperweight led Baccarat to begin a series of sulphides. This series is still being issued at the rate of one or two per year (Fig. 211). The quantities produced varied considerably for the early issues. At present 2,500 regular and 300 overlays of each subject are produced before the die used to form the cameo is permanently defaced.

Much of the sulphide portraiture for these weights has been accomplished by three noted French sculptors: Gilbert Poillerat produced most of the early sulphides, up to and including Martin Luther. He is responsible for the Madonna weight and the continuing zodiac series as well. Miss Dora Mar, a wellknown protegé of Pablo Picasso, crafted the likeness of Churchill. Albert David, official medallist of the French Mint, sculpted the later cameos. The artist's signature and the year the sculpture was created appear on the edge of the sulphide bust, together with the name of the subject (Fig. 210).

In all the tables following, the name of the subject is followed by the name of the artist, the year of issue, and the original prices for both the regular and overlay versions. The colors of the ground or overlay are listed, along with the number of weights produced in each color.

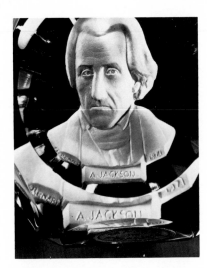

Fig. 210: Above, Detail of Baccarat sulphide showing artist, subject and date. *Fig. 211: Right,* Baccarat sulphides of J. F. Kennedy, Pope Pius XII, Will Rogers and Adlai Stevenson.

PAST LIMITED EDITIONS OF BACCARAT SULPHIDE PAPERWEIGHTS

CORONATION
(G. Poillerat, 1953)

OVERLAY ($75)
Blue 101
Rose 94
                                                    195

REGULAR ($20)
Clear fan 515
Clear diamond .430
Blue 336
Rose 180
Blue diamond 6
Red diamond. 25
                                                    1492

DWIGHT EISENHOWER
(G. Poillerat, 1953)

OVERLAY ($75)
Blue 87
Rose 91
                                                    178

REGULAR ($25)
Blue 366
Clear diamond .189
Rose 173
Clear fan 190
Rose diamond 130
Blue diamond 275
Blue star 39
Rose star 27
                                                    1389

ABRAHAM LINCOLN
(G. Poillerat, 1954)

OVERLAY ($75)
Blue 68
Rose 63
Amethyst. 66
                                                    197

REGULAR ($25)
Clear fan 109
Clear diamond .152
Rose 231
Blue 205
Amethyst 594
                                                    1291

GEORGE WASHINGTON
(G. Poillerat, 1954)

OVERLAY ($75)
Blue 81
Rose 77
Green 42
                                                    200

REGULAR ($25)
Clear fan 96
Clear diamond .115
Rose 301
Blue 280
Green 390
                                                    1182

SIR WINSTON CHURCHILL
(D. Mar, 1954)

OVERLAY ($75)
Blue 39
Rose 29
Amethyst. 13
                                                    81

REGULAR ($25)
Clear. 85
Blue 243
Rose 170
Amethyst. 60
                                                    558

THOMAS JEFFERSON
(G. Poillerat, 1954)

OVERLAY ($75)
Blue 42
Rose 46
Green 68
                                                    156

REGULAR ($25)
Clear fan 46
Clear diamond 54
Rose 194
Blue 201
Rose sand 99
                                                    594

QUEEN ELIZABETH
(G. Poillerat, 1954)

OVERLAY ($75)
White opaline with gold decor 200
                                                    200

ROBERT E. LEE
(D. Mar, 1954)
OVERLAY ($75)
Blue 19
Rose 18
Gray 88
Orange. 11
Flash rose . . . . __1
137

REGULAR ($25)
Clear fan 100
Clear diamond 109
Rose 252
Blue 251
Gray 201
913

BENJAMIN FRANKLIN
(G. Poillerat, 1955)
OVERLAY ($75)
Flash Rose. 180
180
REGULAR ($25)
Clear. 3
Blue 198
Mousse 181
Blue sand. . . . . __32
414

LAFAYETTE
(G. Poillerat, 1955)
OVERLAY ($75)
Lt. blue with clear diamond back 159
Blue with blue sand background . . . . __68
227
REGULAR ($25)
Blue 316
Blue diamond 116
Rose sand 275
Blue star . . . . __37
744

MARTIN LUTHER
(G. Poillerat, 1956)
OVERLAY ($75)
Green with diamond back. . . . . __86
86
REGULAR ($25)
Blue 173
Rose 146
Rose diamond. 179
Blue diamond 100
Red star . . . . __9
607

POPE PIUS XII
(A. David, 1960)
OVERLAY ($100)
White and gold with clear back 131
White and gold with red back 153
284
REGULAR ($30)
Red. 1657
Red star 423
Clear diamond . . . . __77
2157

SAM RAYBURN
(A. David, 1961)
OVERLAY ($100)
Red. 93
93
REGULAR ($30)
Blue 340
Blue star 79
Red. 75
Red star . . . . __18
512

JOHN F. KENNEDY
(A. David, 1964)
OVERLAY ($135)
Rose with blue back. 72
Blue with red back 201
Blue with red star back . . . . __35
308

MEMORIAL
Deep Amethyst 314
314
REGULAR ($35)
Green. 864
Green waffle. .196
Green star 188
Blue 741
Blue waffle 211
Blue star 145
Red. 749
Red waffle 232
Red star 246
3572

POPE JOHN XXIII
(A. David, 1966)
OVERLAY ($145)
Yellow overlay on red back. 190
White opaline flash on yellow back 153
343

REGULAR ($37.50)
Red back 583
Yellow back 192
                  775

THEODORE ROOSEVELT
(A. David, 1967)

OVERLAY ($150)
Gray on green back 359
Gray on clear back 22
                  381

REGULAR ($42.50)
Amethyst back .2359
                2359

WILL ROGERS
(A. David, 1968)

OVERLAY ($150)
Green, clear back, special cutting 383
Blue flash, clear back 6
                  389

REGULAR ($42.50)
Yellow back 2517
                2517

ADLAI STEVENSON
(A. David, 1969)

OVERLAY ($150)
Amethyst on clear back 472
                472

REGULAR ($45)
Orange — red back 2595
                2595

JAMES MONROE
(G. Poillerat, 1970)

OVERLAY ($155)
Green flash with star cut bottom 400
                400

REGULAR ($47.50)
Orange-red ground 2500
                2500

HERBERT HOOVER
(A. David, 1971)

OVERLAY ($155)
Pale Blue 400
                400

REGULAR ($47.50)
Blue back 2500
                2500

ELEANOR ROOSEVELT
(A. David, 1971)

OVERLAY ($155)
Amethyst 400
                400

REGULAR ($47.50)
Amethyst back 2500
                2500

ANDREW JACKSON
(M. Renard, 1972)

OVERLAY ($155)
Green 400
                400

REGULAR ($47.50)
Green back 2400
                2400

WOODROW WILSON
(M. Renard, 1972)

OVERLAY ($160)
Yellow 400
                400

REGULAR ($55)
Light blue back .2400
                2400

HARRY S. TRUMAN
(R. Cochet, 1973)

OVERLAY ($175)
Blue and white 400
                400

REGULAR ($55)
Amber ground 2250
                2250

EVANGELINE HOYSRAD
     BERGSTROM
(R. Cochet, 1973)

REGULAR (ONLY) ($50)
Mauve back, numbered 250
Mauve back, unnumbered 250
                500

GENERAL BONAPARTE (NAPOLEON)
(J. Goy, 1974)

OVERLAY ($175)
Yellow 400
                400

MEMORIAL ($150)
Garnet with red back 100
                100

REGULAR ($60)
Garnet with red back 2000
                2000

Fig. 212: **MODERN BACCARAT.** *Top, No. 1,* Salamander on a sandy yellow ground. *Center row, No. 2,* Patterned millefiori on muslin ground; *No. 3,* Looped garlands on lacy ground. *Bottom row, No. 4,* Gridel rooster. The central figure surrounded by eighteen silhouettes; *No. 5,* Stylized flower with two buds on a color ground.

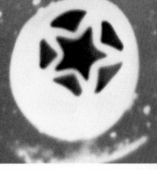

213: Modern Baccarat silhouette, bio.

Fig. 214: Modern Baccarat silhouette, Libra.

Fig. 215: Modern Baccarat stardust cane.

Fig. 216: Modern Baccarat star cane.

In addition to sulphides, modern day Baccarat has developed other traditionally oriented designs (Fig. 212). These include a church weight (Fig. 222) featuring various signs of the zodiac in silhouette (Fig. 213, 214); patterned millefiori; flowers, fruits, snakes, salamanders, and the ongoing Gridel series.

In the Gridel series (Fig. 212, No. 4) each paperweight is highlighted by a large central silhouette representing one of the eighteen historic canes, (Figs. 217-220). Miniature versions of all the original silhouettes are set in various patterned schemes.

The first paperweights in the Gridel series, the rooster and the squirrel, were issued in quantities of 1200: each subsequent edition however, is limited to not more than 350 pieces. For more on the Gridel story see Chapter III.

Fig. 217: Modern Baccarat silhouette cane, butterfly.

GRIDEL ANIMALS PAPERWEIGHT SERIES

(Listed by groups according to the interior color scheme of the silhouette cane.)

White on Black	*Red on White*	*Black on White*	
Pigeon	Devil	Rooster	Monkey (II)
Squirrel		Deer	Elephant
Monkey (I)		Dog	Butterfly
Swan		Goat	Stork
Pheasant		Horse	Pelican
Two birds		Hunter	

Fig. 218: Modern Baccarat silhouette cane, pigeon.

Modern Baccarat Signatures: The Baccarat factory requires that its contemporary products bear the acid-etched stamp of the company. The words "Baccarat, France" appear in a seal with a decanter, a goblet and a tumbler (Fig. 221). Some special limited editions also include a date/signature cane within and have the number of the item on the reverse side.

Fig. 219: Modern Baccarat silhouette cane, dog.

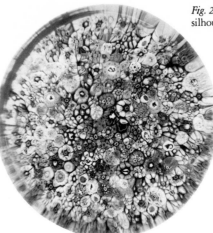

220: Left, Modern Baccarat silhouette — devil. *Fig. 221: Center,* Acid-etched carat signature. *Fig. 222: Right,* Modern Baccarat church weight, featuring zodiac ouettes.

Fig. 223: **MODERN ST. LOUIS.** *Top row, No. 1,* Pears on latticinio. SL 1954; *No. 2,* Clematis within a ring of canes. SL 1954. *Middle row, No. 3,* Double overlay mushroom. SL 1970; *No. 4,* Faceted dahlia. SL 1970. *Bottom row, No. 5,* Marbrie. SL 1971; *No. 6,* Turquoise color ground with patterned millefiori. SL 1972.

St. Louis

St. Louis, one of the three great French factories during the classical paperweight era, resumed production of paperweights after a lapse of nearly 100 years. Their contemporary output of both millefiori and sulphide weights is detailed below (Figs. 223, 224, 225, 226, 234).

Millefiori: St. Louis began experimenting with modern millefiori weights in 1950; production continued through 1955. At that time commercial production ceased, and was not resumed until 1970. The most recent efforts began at the coaxing of Paul Jokelson, who also got Baccarat sulphide production off to a new start. These new St. Louis weights are patterned, for the most part, on the classic antique designs. They are distributed primarily in the United States, although some are now sold in France and England. Examples of modern St. Louis millefiori canes are pictured in Figs. 227, 228, 229.

Modern St. Louis identification: Florets are contained in all editions issued by the factory since 1970. The cane features both date and signature in a single floret (Figs. 230, 231). Commemorative sulphides are usually signed on the reverse of the cameo (Figs. 232, 233), or on the base of the weight with the acid-etched stamp of the factory. Modern editions are also accompanied by a certificate.

: 1973-1974 ST. LOUIS. *Top row, No. 1,* Flower with bud; looped garland. *Bottom row, No. 3,* Crown; *No. 4,* Flower with

Fig. 225: 1975 ST. LOUIS. *Top row, No. 1,* Hawaiian millefiori; *No. 2,* Double overlay bouquet. *No. 3,* Cherries in a basket; *No. 4,* Pom Pom or camomile on latticinio.

MODERN ST. LOUIS MILLEFIORI PAPERWEIGHTS

Fig. 226: St. Louis 1972 piedouche.

Fig. 227: Modern St. Louis millefiori cane.

Fig. 228: Modern St. Louis millefiori cane.

Fig. 229: Modern St. Louis millefiori cane.

Year	Item	Number Made
1970	**MUSHROOM OVERLAY:** A millefiori mushroom set in clear glass within a blue, red, or pistachio double overlay. A plain white overlay was also issued.	100 ea. color
	DAHLIA: A large flowerhead in blue, red, or pistachio fills the weight.	150 ea. color
	CLEMATIS: A red or pistachio flower and bud with stems and leaves is set in a dark ground.	150 ea. color
1971	**MARBRIE:** This weight is very similar to the antique St. Louis marbrie, in tones of blue, pistachio and white.	250
	PINWHEEL: Similar to the Clichy swirl, but with the design very high in the dome. Issued in blue-and-white and multicolor.	250 ea. comb.
	FLAT BOUQUET: Red, blue, and pistachio colored clematis flowers set on a white ground.	250
	STAR MILLEFIORI: Star-shaped millefiori on a white ground in a close patterned weight.	180
	STAR MILLEFIORI OVERLAY: Issued only in Europe, this weight is an overlay version of the "Star millefiori" weight described above.	
1972-3	**CARPET GROUND:** Five circles of green millefiori are set into a light pink carpet ground.	250
	DOILY: Patterned millefiori in the shape of a doily on a translucent blue ground.	250
	TURQUOISE COLOR GROUND: Parallel rods of lace dividing millefiori canes are set into a rich color ground.	250
	BLUE AND WHITE CARPET GROUND: Closely packed cogwheel·canes with white rims and blue centers surround a single central green complex floret.	250
	FLOWER ON LATTICINIO: A revival of a favorite backdrop supports a light blue clematis with a bud.	250
	PIEDOUCHE: A close millefiori or concentric millefiori subject rests on a rimmed latticinio foot. This weight is similar to one produced in 1953. St. Louis expects to make this weight in small editions every five years.	

| 1973-4 | CROWN: A multicolored crown weight similar to the antique variety first popularized by St. Louis. | 250 |

(See Fig. 195) CANE FLOWER: A flower with five rounded-cane petals rests on a stem with green leaves and a bud. Produced with either an orange or a pistachio ground. — 250 ea. color

LOOPED MILLEFIORI: Looped millefiori garlands set on a blood-red ground. — 250

PEN HOLDER: A striped latticinio vase rests on a concentric millefiori paperweight base. — 125

1974 HONEYCOMB: Millefiori canes in tones of red are arranged high in the dome to give a honey-comb effect. — 250

NEWEL POST: A large newel post completely filled with millefiori and fitted out in high-polish brass. — 250

WHITE DAHLIA: A flower composed of numerous long white petals which overlap is supported by a green stem with two leaves and is set on a mauve ground. — 250

1975 (See Fig. 196) HAWAIIAN MILLEFIORI: Patterned after brightly-colored Hawaiian fabric, the weight features rows of colorful, stylized floral canes. — 250

DOUBLE OVERLAY BOUQUET: A red and a white clematis on green stems are set in clear glass within a blue and white overlay. — 250

CHERRY WEIGHT: Numerous red cherries on delicate stems with green leaves are set on a swirling latticinio ground in this faceted paperweight. — 250

POM POM or CAMOMILE: A full-blown flower is supported by a stem with two green leaves and rests on a latticinio ground. — 250

Fig. 230: Modern St. Louis signature/date cane.

Fig. 231: Modern St. Louis signature/date cane.

Fig. 232: Detail, commemorative St. Louis sulphide.

Fig. 233: Detail, commemorative St. Louis sulphide.

Millefiori weights produced by St. Louis during their "early" modern period (1950-1955) include the following types:

Piedouche
Upright bouquet on latticinio
Clematis with ring of canes
Mixed fruit on latticinio
Cherries

Lemons
Mixed vegetables
Double Flower bouquet
Mushroom overlay

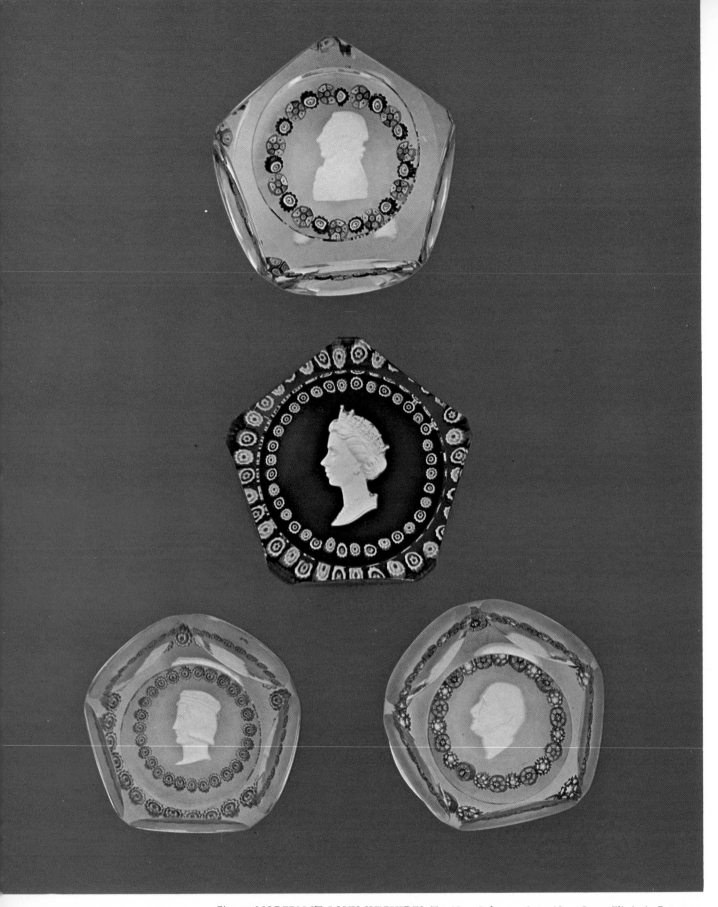

Fig. 234: **MODERN ST. LOUIS SULPHIDES.** *Top, No. 1,* Lafayette. *Center, No. 2,* Queen Elizabeth. *Bottom row, No. 3,* King of France; *No. 4,* President Schuman.

Sulphide Paperweights: (Fig. 234) St. Louis began producing a small but quite successful series of sulphide paperweights in 1953. Between 1955 and 1970 the factory manufactured this type of paperweight only. An edition of 1226 paperweights commemorating Queen Elizabeth's coronation was their first modern achievement in this field. A ring of millefiori canes frequently surrounds the subject. Some of these weights have an "SL 1953" cane among those making up the millefiori garland; all bear the circular inscription "COURONNEMENT 2-6-53 ST LOUIS FRANCE" on the base. Although the issue price of the weights was a mere $18 to $20, they are worth over ten times this amount on today's market.

ST. LOUIS CORONATION SULPHIDES
(Type of ground and number of each produced are shown.)

Clear crystal	47
Clear crystal with millefiori	132
Turquoise	60
Turquoise with millefiori	324
Red	71
Red with millefiori	118
Dark blue	57
Dark blue with millefiori	290
Black	2
Topaz with millefiori	2
Red jasper	61
Blue jasper	62

St. Louis followed up the Queen Elizabeth sulphide with a small series of cameo paperweights aimed primarily at the French market. They were all produced with clear glass grounds and with a ring of millefiori canes encircling the cameo portrait.

MODERN ST. LOUIS SULPHIDES

Year:	Item:	Number Made:
1967	GENERAL FRANCOIS INGOLD	9
1967	SAINT LOUIS, KING OF FRANCE: Made in honor of the 200th anniversary of the founding of the St. Louis factory. Signed in blue letters on the back of the sulphide "1767-SL-1967". A set of twenty overlay versions was issued.	2000
1967	LAFAYETTE: Made for the directors and friends of the Paris department store, Galeries Lafayette. This weight was not signed.	250
1969	PRESIDENT ROBERT SCHUMAN: Commissioned by friends of Robert Schuman, this weight was marked on the base with the acid-etched factory seal. Written in blue on the back of the cameo are the initials "R.S." and the dates "1886-1963".	300

Fig. 235: **MODERN D'ALBRET SULPHIDES.** *Top, No. 1,* John F. and Jacqueline Kennedy overlay. *Second row, No. 2,* H.R.H. Prince Charles; *No. 3,* Leonardo da Vinci. *Center, No. 4,* Ernest Hemingway overlay. *Third row, No. 5,* General Douglas MacArthur; *No. 6,* Franklin D. Roosevelt. *Bottom, No. 7,* Paul Revere overlay.

Cristalleries Et Verreries De Vianne (Cristal D'Albret) (Fig. 235)

Glassmaking first came to the town of Vianne, France when the Cristalleries et Verreries de Vianne was organized by Mr. Roger Witkind in 1918. In 1967, with Paul Jokelson of New York again providing the stimulus, the factory inaugurated a series of sulphide paperweights under the name "Cristalleries d'Albret." At this time the 800-worker factory already had a good reputation in the glass industry.

D'Albret sulphides are issued in both regular and overlay editions and are distributed primarily in the United States. Single, double, and flash overlays have all been successfully produced. The faceting is identical on all weights of the same subject. Only one color or color combination is utilized with each subject, although shades may vary from weight to weight.

The first artist employed to make the cameos for these paperweights was George Simon. He is well known for his engravings for the French mint, and has won a number of awards for his artistry. M. Simon crafted the sculptures for the first four paperweights issued by d'Albret: Christopher Columbus, Franklin Roosevelt, the King of Sweden, and John F. and Jaqueline Kennedy. This last was produced in an edition of only 121 pieces due to an accident at the factory in which the mold was broken. It is referred to as the "experimental overlay." It was at this point that Gilbert Poillerat, an engraver for the French government who had also done extensive sulphide work for Baccarat, was called upon. He agreed to craft sulphides for the rest of the series, including another likeness of the Kennedys.

D'Albret Signatures: These weights are signed using an acid-etching process on the base of the weight (Fig. 236). The inscription, in a circle of printed letters, reads "CR. ALBRET — FRANCE". Furthermore, each sulphide subject is signed on the edge of the bust with the name of the subject, the date the sculpture was made, and the initials of the artist (Fig. 237). A certificate accompanies each weight.

Fig. 236: Above, Cristal d'Albret acid-etched signature. *Fig. 237: Right,* Detail of sulphide showing artist, date and subject.

D'ALBRET SULPHIDES

Subject	Artist	Date	Number of Regulars	Number of Overlays
Christopher Columbus	G.S.	1966	1000	200
F. D. Roosevelt	G.S.	1967	2000	300
J. F. and Mrs. Kennedy	G.S.	1967	2000	121 experimental
H. M. Gustaf VI Adolf K. of Sweden	G.S.	1967	1000	none
J. F. and Mrs. Kennedy	G.P.	1969	none	300
Leonardo da Vinci	G.P.	1968	1000	200
Douglas MacArthur	G.P.	1968	1000	225
Mark Twain	G.P.	1969	1000	225
Ernest Hemingway	G.P.	1969	1000	225
Paul Revere	G.P.	1969	800	200
Albert Schweitzer	G.P.	1969	1000	200
H.R.H. Prince Charles	G.P.	1970	1000	200
Moon astronauts	G.P.	1971	1000	225
John J. Audubon	G.P.	1972	1000	225
Jenny Lind	G.P.	1973	410	170
David Ben Gurion	G.P.	1973	750	150
Golda Meir	G.P.	1974	850	150

Fig. 238: John J. Audubon.

Perthshire Paperweights (Figs. 239, 240, 257)

In the mid-1960s Vasart Glass of Perth, Scotland (refer to section on Paul Ysart) was producing a line of vases, ashtrays, and paperweights. Insolvency loomed, however, and aid was sought from a local lawyer, Stuart Drysdale. Drysdale came up with some money and also with new work: contract from Wm. Teacher & Sons, the distillers, for ashtrays made from old bottles. The Scottish brewers, however, aspired to move from their status as big customer to one of big shareholder. They acquired the company, renamed it Strathearn Glass, and moved it to a new site in Crieff. This new arrangement did not please Drysdale or the company's leading artisans. After an unsuccessful attempt to buy back the company in 1968, Drysdale and the master glassblowers left and founded Perthshire Paperweights.

At first they worked in an old schoolhouse which had been converted into a make-shift factory. In only two years, however, their tremendous success in the field of limited edition collectors' paperweights enabled them to open a new factory in Crieff in January of 1971. The factory presently employs 25 persons. It is devoted entirely to the production of millefiori paperweights and related articles. It is probably the only factory in the world committed exclusively to this type of work.

Jack Allan, Perthshire's master glassman, has worked in this field for over 25 years. He is rated by Mr. Drysdale as probably the best man in the world at this work. Anton Moravec, who received his training in Czechoslovakia, is in charge of cutting and faceting. His excellent work enhances many of the millefiori and floral designs. With these two experts overseeing the technical aspects of production, the quality of Perthshire paperweights continues to improve.

The "metal" (glass) is produced in a one-ton tank on the weekends for work during the ensuing week. Almost all of the raw materials used in its manufacture are from local sources. Only the coloring agents are imported but the factory is now working toward producing its own color. The Perthshire glass is not particularly high in lead content. It is consequently not heavy, but it compares favorably with other paperweight glass in terms of clarity and brightness.

Millefiori designs are created by the workmen themselves. They are encouraged to develop a feeling for glass by experimenting with colors and motifs. About one-third of the working time is spent on the manufacture of individual millefiori canes.

The factory issues three series of paperweights: special limited editions, which are produced once and not again; regular limited editions, made in small numbers but repeated each year with the appropriate date cane included; and decorative weights, always in production. This last category is the bread-and-butter line, financing production of the time-consuming limited editions. Even so, they are probably the best decorative weights on the market. They should not be considered collectors' pieces, however.

Fig. 239: **PERTHSHIRE.** *Top row, No. 1,* Swan in a pond. *Middle row, No. 2.* Miniature flower floating over a basket of pulled millefiori canes; *No. 3,* Mistletoe Christmas weight. *Bottom row, No. 4,* Close pack millefiori; *No. 5,* Blue clematis flower resting on a latticinio ground.

Fig. 240: **PERTHSHIRE LIMITED EDITIONS.** *Top row, No. 1,* Double overlay with close pack motif; *No. 2,* Bouquet with hovering dragonfly. *Center, No. 3,* Miniature faceted flower. *Bottom row, No. 4,* White flower with two buds; *No. 5,* Spaced millefiori on translucent blue ground.

Although simple millefiori production weights can be made at the rate of approximately 80 per day, the special limited editions sometimes take up to ten months to complete. Consequently, quantities of limited editions are determined by production parameters rather than potential demand projections. Only as many as may be reasonably made in six to ten months are produced. New designs are always being created at Perthshire. Workers want to keep the tedium of producing the same weight over and over to a minimum. Approximately 45% of the paperweights produced are exported, primarily to the United States.

Silhouette canes: The Scottish factory has recently added silhouette canes to their annual limited editions of paperweights using scattered millefiori on lace. Subjects of the new canes include: (Figs. 244-253)

Polar bear	Owl	*(not pictured)*
Jumping rabbit	Cat	Deer
Duck	Scotty dog	Rooster
Penguin	Pelican	
Sailboat	Donkey	

Perthshire Dating: From their beginning in 1969, the Perthshire management has realized the importance of signing and dating all fine quality pieces while their inexpensive decorative weights are not signed. Methods that have been used include initialling with a diamond stylus and the use of various types of signature canes (Figs. 241, 242, 243). Typical geometric canes from Perthshire are pictured in Figs. 254, 255, 256.

An alphabetical system is used in some limited editions: the letter A represents 1969, the first year of paperweight manufacture at Perthshire, and subsequent letters are assigned to each year thereafter. A few weights have been issued with the initials of Jack Allen (J.A.), the master glassblower at Perthshire, and those of Anton Moravec (A.M.), who does the faceting (Fig. 258).

Fig. 241   *Fig. 242*   *Fig. 243*

Fig. 244

241, 242, 243: Perthshire signature canes. *Fig. 244:* Polar bear. *Fig. 245:* Running rabbit. *Fig. 246:*
k. *Fig. 247:* Penguin. *Fig. 248:* Sailboat. *Fig. 249:* Owl. *Fig. 250:* Cat. *Fig. 251:* Scotty dog. *Fig. 252:*
:an. *Fig. 253:* Donkey. *Figs. 254, 255, 256:* Typical Perthshire geometric cane.

245   Fig. 246   Fig. 247   Fig. 248

249   Fig. 250   Fig. 251   Fig. 252

253   Fig. 254   Fig. 255   Fig. 256

121

Fig. 257: **PERTHSHIRE.** *Top row, No. 1,* Faceted patterned millefiori signed in the central cane "B" for the second year of manufacture (1970); *No. 2,* Spaced millefiori on lace, containing two silhouettes and a date/signature cane "P 1972". *Second row, No. 3,* Faceted pansy on lace, surrounded by a garland of canes; *No. 4,* Dragonfly with delicate lace wings, in a wreath of millefiori canes. *Center, No. 5,* Miniature flower floating above a stave basket. *Bottom row, No. 6.* Translucent green overlay weight; *No. 7,* Faceted "cushion" weight.

PERTHSHIRE SPECIAL LIMITED EDITIONS

Date	Item	Number Made
1969	CROWN: Red, white, and blue canes. Similar to the type made by St. Louis in the 19th century, but not hollow. Dated P1969 on base.	350
1970:	DRAGONFLY: Dragonfly suspended in clear glass surrounded by a garland of composite canes. Signed with diamond pen on base: P1970.	150
	FLASH OVERLAY: Pattern of six floating composite florets in flash overlay. Signed J.A. and A.M. P1970 in script on base. Six different colors were used.	150
1971:	FLASH OVERLAY BOTTLE: Two shades of amethyst on highly faceted bottle with millefiori base. Signed as above: P1971.	300
	RIBBON: Series of upright ribbons meeting at the top in a cane containing a small rose. Signed at the base: JA.	150
	FACETED PANSY: Pansy surrounded by garland of composite canes on latticinio ground. Signed on base: P1971.	350
	CUSHION: A complex pattern of composite millefiori canes on a velvet cushion base of varying colors. Signed P1971 on base.	250
	CHRISTMAS HOLLY: Sprig of holly leaves and berries on upset muslin.	250
1972	FACETED CUSHION: Similar to that made in 1971, but faceted to match the millefiori pattern. Signed on base: P1972.	300
	DAHLIA: A faceted weight containing a dahlia with four layers of pink petals. Signed on base: P1972.	200
	MINIATURE FLOWER: Small pink flower floating in a basket of composite canes, the center of the flower bearing the factory signature "P".	1000
	CHRISTMAS MISTLETOE WEIGHT: Sprig of the merriest plant surrounded by a garland of green and white canes and set on a brilliant red background. Signed P1972 on base.	300

1973	FLOWER IN BASKET WEIGHT: A five-petaled blue clematis with green leaves and stem on a latticinio ground. Signed "P" in center of flower.	300
	CLOSE MILLEFIORI: A close pack millefiori containing a selection of complex canes, one with the date/signature P1973.	400
	SWAN IN THE POND: A replica of the old weight but signed with the factory initial on the wing of the swan. Heavily faceted.	250
1974	LARGE BOUQUET: A dragonfly hovers above a three-flower bouquet consisting of two clematis flowers and a pansy (bearing the factory signature). The bouquet is tied with a yellow ribbon. The clear glass setting is faceted with large windows.	300
	DOUBLE OVERLAY: Closely packed complex millefiori canes, including a date cane, are set in a deep amethyst ground. The purple and white double overlay is faceted with sixteen side printies and a large top window.	300
	FACETED MINIATURE FLOWER: A small five-petal flower bearing the factory signature cane as its stamen is set in clear crystal. The base is strawberry cut.	600
	FLOWER WITH BUDS: A white clematis with dark tips on a stem with two white buds is set on a lilac ground.	350
	MILLEFIORI GARLAND: A patterned millefiori design centered on a flower silhouette cane is set on a brightly-colored opaque cushion.	350
1975	TUDOR ROSE: A magnum weight containing a central red rose with a spiraling stalk and leaves, all within a garland of millefiori canes. Blue ground.	400
	MILLEFIORI CIRCLETS ON A CUSHION: Six millefiori clusters, surrounded by a garland of canes, are set on a brightly colored cushion.	400
	PENGUIN WEIGHT: The subject of this translucent ice blue overlay paperweight is a penguin on an ice flow. The weight is hollow-centered and deeply faceted.	350
	BUTTERFLY WEIGHT: The insect, wings spread within a garland of millefiori, is perched on a ribbed and brightly-colored cushion.	

Fig. 258: Perthshire overlay bottle.

124

OVERLAY BOTTLE: A flash overlay
bottle of unusual shape with a millefiori base
and matching stopper.

Mr. Drysdale of Perthshire states: "It is not our business to insure the collector an appreciating investment, but we are very concerned to see that he (or she) gets value for his (or her) money." Despite this disclaimer, Perthshire paperweights, as they come ever closer to the quality of the French classics, are already showing signs of being the "antiques of the future."

Whitefriars

Production has recently been increased with the gift market in mind. Weights from these recent large issues may not have the same value, from a collector's standpoint, as their earlier counterparts.

Chinese Paperweights

Sometime in the early 1930's, a selection of antique French and American paperweights was taken to China by an unidentified importer for the purpose of having them copied. The concept of a glass dome-shaped paperweight was new at that time to the Chinese, who used rectangular carved pieces of jade instead. Glassblowing and lampworking, however, had a long history in China, and arranging a production scheme for the copying of paperweights was deemed feasible (Fig. 259).

Glass factories located in Shantung Province had made glass novelties and parts for glass flowers, but apparently had never been exposed to millefiori manufacturing techniques. Perhaps this is why the canes used in these early weights are rather simplistic in design. Chinese color schemes predominate. Red, bright yellow, orange, and green elements make these weights easily distinguishable. Another clue to origin is the yellowish cast which taints the glass in almost all early examples. Special care seems to have been taken to develop a number of designs, but these were subsequently mass-produced with little quality control; consequently, they vary greatly in quality.

The best early weights were perhaps those copied directly from Western examples. They were finished with concave bases. Copies of American designs often had the quatrefoil faceting typical of the New England Glass Company. These early "copies" included the following:

    Baccarat primrose — yellow flower overlaid with orange petals
    American double clematis or poinsettia
    NEGC nosegay — surrounded by two rows of canes on a latticinio ground; quatrefoil cutting

Fig. 259: **OLD CHINESE PAPERWEIGHTS.** *Top, No. 1,* Imitation of a Millville rose. *Top left, No. 2,* Imitation of a Baccarat pansy. *Center, No. 3,* Orange flower head on latticinio. *Top right, No. 4,* Imitation of N.E.G.C. nosegay with quatrefoil faceting. *Lower left, No. 5,* painted weight with Chinese motif. *Bottom, No. 6,* Scrambled millefiori with the signature plaque "Made in China." *Lower right, No. 7,* Two orange blossoms on tree branch, all resting on lace ground.

Fig. 260: **MODERN CHINESE PAPERWEIGHTS.** *Top, No. 1,* Peacock. *Top left, No. 2,* Footed tulip. *Top right, No. 3,* Three birds on green leaves, a footed weight. *Upper center, No. 4,* Millefiori cane tree. *Center left, No. 5,* Poinsettia Christmas weight, with Chinese characters. *Center right, No. 6,* Pink flower. *Lower center, No. 7,* Yellow and red primrose. *Bottom left, No. 8, and bottom right, No. 9,* Painted Chinese heads. *Bottom, No. 10,* Upright blue flower.

St. Louis upright bouquet — on a latticinio ground; attached to the ground and extending
 across the dome is a spiral filigree handle making a basket for the flowers
Baccarat pansy — on clear and latticinio grounds
Millville roses — in various colors

Other less impressive designs were also manufactured. Concentric and scrambled millefiori were made in great quantity. A few designs reflect originality on the part of the Chinese workmen, such as the motif of two orange blossoms on a stylized branch, for instance, or a painted weight featuring a maiden in a pastoral setting. Inkwells or perfume bottles similar to English examples, with scrambled or concentric millefiori in stopper and base, were also made as well as upright flowers reminiscent of modern mid-western American designs. They also manufactured millefiori chopstick holders, glass cubes, pyramids, and other geometric shapes housing glass or sulphide birds, monkeys, or other representational elements.

Some of the early Chinese scrambled millefiori weights contain a small rectangular plaque reading "MADE IN CHINA" (Fig. 269). Others were designated with paper labels or had "China" etched in script on the base (Fig. 270).

Chinese paperweight manufacturers have been active in the past decade and many new designs have been added to their lines of export glass (Fig. 260). Notable examples of original work include large doorstop weights containing realistic green lilies with one or two frogs poised for a leap and a variety of other floral scenes replete with butterflies, dragonflies, etc.

An interesting Chinese application of the millefiori technique is the use of a number of feather-like canes arranged in a close-packed design representing the tail of a peacock: the head is pressed into the top of the weight and the bottom side is ground flat, allowing the piece to stand vertically as a strutting bird. (See Fig. 260, No. 1) Feather canes are also found in other millefiori designs. Typical Chinese millefiori canes are pictured in Figs. 261-266.

One modern Chinese paperweight exhibiting a unique blend of Eastern and Western elements features a red Christmas poinsettia with "Peace On Earth" written in Chinese ideograms borne on four canes (Figs. 267, 268).

Cubic, rectangular, and animal-shaped millefiori paperweights are also being produced. The cubes, which contain upright figures of birds or animals, show the mastery of the art of enclosing glass figures within clear glass (Fig. 271). The glass used in these weights is quite light in heft, but it is much clearer than that used in the early Chinese paperweights.

Author's Note on Collecting Chinese Paperweights: For those who have little money to spare for paperweight collecting, Chinese paperweights offer a somewhat unusual, colorful, and definitely inexpensive alternative. When Chinese paperweights first appeared in the United States, for example, they sold between 25¢ and $2.00; prices F.O.B. Hong Kong haven't risen much since then, although some older or peculiar pieces now command higher prices. It's interesting to note that at least two paperweight dealers, these authors included, find Chinese paperweights interesting to collect.

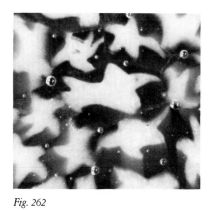

Fig. 262

Fig. 263

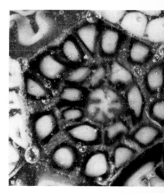

Fig. 264

Fig. 266

Fig. 267

Fig. 268

Fig. 261: Chinese feather cane. Fig. 262: Chinese star cane. Fig. 263: Typical Chinese geometrical cane. Fig. 264: Typical Chinese geometrical cane. Fig. 265: Typical Chinese serrated cane. Fig. 266: Silhouette canes, two birds and flower. Fig. 267: "Peace" in Chinese characters. Fig. 268: "World" or "Earth" in Chinese characters. Fig. 269: Chinese signature plaque. Fig. 270: Chinese script signature. Fig. 271: Cube weight, waterfowl in reeds.

Fig. 270

Fig. 271

Fig. 272: **FRANCIS WHITTEMORE.** *Top row, No. 1,* Iowa state flower, the wild rose; *No. 2,* Butterfly over a bouquet. *Middle row, No. 3,* Bouquet; *No. 4,* Cane dahlia bouquet. *Bottom row, No. 5,* Mushrooms; *No. 6,* Pears.

Chapter V

The Paperweight Renaissance — The Studio Artists

Francis Dyer Whittemore, Jr.

Creating miniaturized and stylized glass reproductions of nature began as an adolescent hobby and became a lifelong occupation for Francis Whittemore. Although he was born in Hackensack, New Jersey (on January 6, 1921), Whittemore's family moved shortly thereafter to Massachusetts. It was at Harvard University that he saw the famous glass flower collection — an experience that led him to a number of domestic experiments with bunsen burner and glass rods. He became so proficient that by the time he was in high school he was supplying goblets, decanters, and scaled-down (1′ = 1″) animal figurines to local gift shops.

After high school Whittemore studied at Harvard for two years before entering the military. Following his discharge in 1946, he spent sixteen years as a technical glassblower for two large American firms and eventually became a teacher at the Salem County Vocational Technical Institute in Salem County, New Jersey. It was there that, in 1962, a student's question about paperweight manufacturing techniques led Whittemore to look into the subject.

Whittemore's first five years as a paperweight-maker were largely consumed in increasingly successful efforts to duplicate the deceptively simple-looking Millville rose. Although much smaller than earlier footed rose paperweights, Whittemore's creations are just as beautiful and, perhaps, more delicate. Whittemore roses have also been successfully incorporated into perfume bottles, cruets, glasses, and other small objects (Fig. 274).

In 1967, having conquered the Millville rose, Whittemore decided that it was time to take up a new challenge: his work would rival the classic French paperweights.

At first his efforts were only mildly triumphant. His 1967-1969 paperweight production is characterized by white, pink, or clear grounds; flat floral and fruit subjects; and very low domes. After two years of experimental work, however, Whittemore produced a number of pieces which were astonishingly better than anything he had done before. Weights made after 1969 reflect the highest degree of technical skill and artistic excellence (Figs. 272, 275).

Whittemore presently resides in Lansdale, Pennsylvania. Having gone into business for himself in 1968, he has built many of his own tools and developed his own techniques of glass manufacture. Some of the subjects issued thus far in limited editions are single flowers, bouquets, and Christmas motifs. A series of state flowers is being produced in editions of 100 pieces and will, of course, take many years to complete. Whittemore limited editions are issued with a numbered certificate and all weights are signed with a "W" cane inside the weight on the reverse of the motif (Fig. 273).

WHITTEMORE PAPERWEIGHTS

Subjects of Limited Editions

Bleeding heart
Butterfly on a bouquet
California poppy
Christmas stocking (1972)
Colorado columbine
Fuchsia
Hummingbird
Iowa rose
Minnesota lady slipper
North Carolina and Virginia dogwood
Pedestal nosegay
South Carolina jessamine

Other French-Style Paperweights Issued in Small Quantities

Acorn
Bouquets
Christmas candles
Dahlia, various colors
Holly
Lily-of-the-valley
Mushrooms
Pansy
Partridge in a pear tree
Pears
Rose
Violet

Fig. 273: Whittemore signature cane.

Fig. 274: Whittemore perfume bottle.

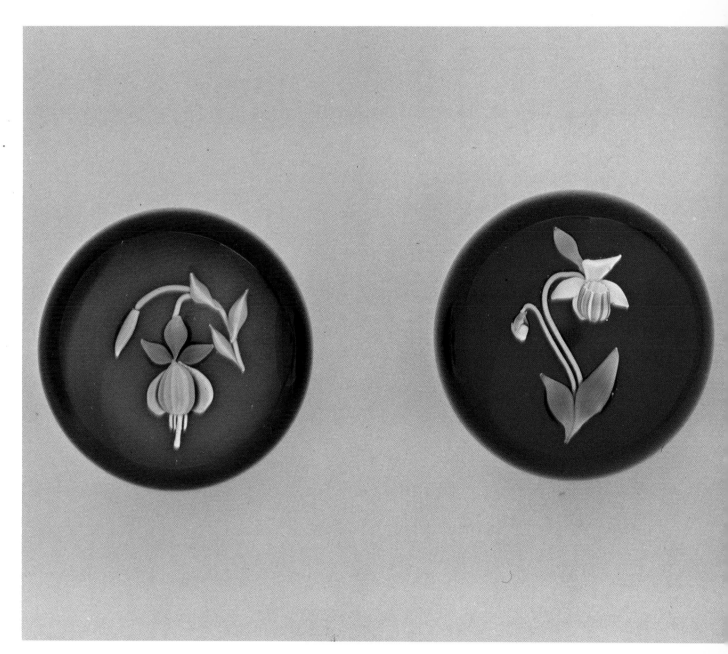

Fig. 275: Whittemore fuchsia and lady slipper.

Paul Joseph Stankard

Paul Stankard of Mantua, New Jersey, combines a background in scientific glass-blowing with a keen interest in art glass. During a ten year stint in industrial work, he became fascinated with antique and modern paperweights. Now that he has decided to make his formerly avocational glass artistry a full-time occupation, he can call himself a "contemporary American floral paperweight maker" — a title he has long desired. (Figs. 277, 278)

A visit to the Ware Collection of Blaschka Glass Models of Plants at Harvard University was one of the stimuli resulting in Paul's interest in floral paperweights. Constantly searching for originality and realism within this art form, he is currently pursuing a series of floral designs. Each design has been or will be issued in editions limited to between 50 and 75 paperweights. His motifs, the products of many hours of experimentation, exhibit features rarely, if ever found, in antique or contemporary paperweights. He has developed intricate veining on petals and leaves, finely detailed upright stamens, and delicate root systems. Perhaps because of their faithfulness to Mother Nature, Stankard weights are always graceful and artistic. They are easily identified by the "S" or "PS" canes they contain, or by a script signature and number etched on the side or base of the weight (Fig. 276).

STANKARD PAPERWEIGHTS

Motif: *Number Made:*

Floral Series

Dogwood 75
Lady slipper 50
Merry bell 75
Orchid 75
Poinsettia 50
Spring beauty 50
White marsh gentian 75
Bell wort 75

Medicinal Herb Series

Cayenne pepper 50
Goat's rue 50
Red plantain 50

Non-Limited Paperweights

Flaming glory	Meadow wreath	Strawberry
Forget-me-not	Red maid	Painted trillium

Fig. 277 (far right): Paul Stankard meadow wreath. *Fig. 276 (right):* Stankard signature cane.

Fig. 278: **PAUL JOSEPH STANKARD.** *Top row, No. 1,* Magnolia on vine with many buds; *No. 2,* Miniature striped clematis. *Middle row, No. 3,* Lady slipper; *No. 4,* Spring beauty with root system. *Bottom row, No. 5,* Clematis with four buds; *No. 6,* Flower with complex stamen and stem system.

Fig. 279: **CHARLES KAZIUN PAPERWEIGHTS.** *Top row, No. 1,* Red rose and bud within a torsade of twi
lace on blue on blue ground; *No. 2,* Spangled red poinsettia on white ground. *Second row, No. 3,* Arrow cane flo
resting on pink ground; *No. 4,* Striped snake coiled around a red rose, all set on yellow jasper ground; *No. 5,* Cor
vulous or morning glory and bud on a trellis. *Bottom row, No. 6,* Pansy and bud on an apricot colored jasper gro
No. 7, Four stylized roses resting on five leaves.

Charles Kaziun (Fig. 279)

The first twentieth-century glass craftsman to produce French style paperweights of fine quality, Charles Kaziun has brought new designs and techniques to the art glass field during a lifelong career (Figs. 280, 281). Not that there haven't been obstacles, production-related and otherwise.

Perhaps the first hurdle was convincing his parents to contribute the daily admission price ($1) to the annual Brockton Fair so that he could observe the Howell family of glass workers give their demonstrations of lampworked art glass. "I was watching every movement and operation . . . " he later admitted. Indeed, the Howells eventually refused to perform further demonstrations under his continuous scrutiny. This second barrier was overcome with characteristic ingenuity: Kaziun got a job in the fair booth across the way. Although his ambition during high school was to become a chemist, he experimented at home with old broken bottles rather than with acids and bases. His melting pots were old cans and his choice ingredients the result of scavenging operations; he claims nevertheless that some of these early pieces "succeeded rather well."

Kaziun got a production glass job in New York after his graduation from high school, but the employment was short-lived and emphasized "efficiency" rather than artistry. After one of those gray periods of scraping by, Kaziun succeeded in getting a job with — the Howells! They were perfectionists like Charles, and they were instructing him to produce beautiful work, not just to go faster. "In addition to the regular exhibition work, I was permitted to do much creative experimentation in free time," Kaziun later recalled. He began to make buttons as much for fun and expression as for profit.

One button got as far afield as James D. Graham, a biologist and scientific glass-blower at the University of Pennsylvania. When the two men met in 1942, Kaziun was offered an instrument-making position at UP and accepted. It was shortly after this that a reading of Evangeline Bergstrom's classic *Old Glass Paperweights* sparked Kaziun's initial interest in antique French weights. Graham became a sympathetic but demanding mentor to Kaziun, countering the artist's recurrent self-doubt with encouragement while calling attention to imperfections which sometimes Kaziun himself did not perceive. The accepted formula for this interpersonal chemistry was "Your work is good, but the French . . . " Graham carried out a patron's most important function: his continuing interest in Kaziun's work gave the artist the moral support required for the endless hours of experimentation needed to approach the quality of antique French paperweights. This was challenge enough until a wartime acquaintanceship with Emil Larson, introduced Kaziun to the Millville rose.

"You've tackled a tough one," Graham is reported to have said to Kaziun near the outset of his four-year $3,000 attempt to produce a perfect Millville bloom. The Kaziun rose is now perhaps as famed among collectors as its alluring prototype, but, none have been produced for many years now. Kaziun has, however, hinted that he may make a few more. In any event, they are a worthy addition to any paperweight collection.

Meanwhile, Kaziun encountered continuing difficulties with obtaining high quality ingredients for his glass. Obtaining compatible clear and colored glass was one problem that had to be solved. Although Kaziun found a good European supplier for colored glass, he felt constrained to manufacture his own clear crystal. A glass with a high lead content, such as that used by St. Louis and Baccarat, was ruled out in favor of non-leaded glass, because the latter would have brilliance but would not be as prone to striations. This type of glass is found in many Clichy weights. The procurement of the highest-quality material is not a problem that can be "solved," and Kaziun still worries over it: "Colors in paperweights must be quite rich, and I believe the door is shutting on available sources for these rich colors," he has warned.

For the rest, Charles Kaziun has somehow figured out a way to single-handedly manufacture millefiori canes which are usually the creation of a team of two to four persons. The miniscule "K" canes with which he signs his millefiori creations begins as approximately a ¼″ diameter rod and is pulled out to 6′ in length, because, accord-

Fig. 280: Three footed weights and perfume bottle by Kaziun.

ing to Kaziun, that is his armspan. He has also perfected a fine muslin and a swirling latticinio for use as grounds in floral and cane weights.

Some of the more famous flora in Kaziun lampwork paperweights are: rose, tulip, daffodil, lily, pansy, dogwood, poinsettia, morning glory (convolvulus) and crocus. A miniature spider lily set on various grounds and given a pedestal is one of his most popular pieces; it, like the rose motif, has been used in perfume bottles.

One of Kaziun's greatest triumphs (and tribulations) is his triple overlay paperweight. He states that, whereas he has about a 50/50 chance of making a good single overlay, his success factor in a triple overlay drops to one in nine!

Kaziun weights are all signed with either a 14k gold "K" and/or a millefiori "K" signature cane worked into the design (Fig. 282). Some of his flower weights contain a tiny gold bumblebee hovering over the blossom. In fact, gold foil enclosures have been included in many paperweights and buttons over the years.

Kaziun's canes, appearing in spaced millefiori paperweights and a number of paperweight buttons, are usually set on a color ground frequently containing gold flecks. Subjects include (Figs. 283, 284):

Clover	Rabbit
Duck	Signature cane
Goose	Turtle
Heart	Rose
Horse head	Stardust

Fig. 281: Kaziun millefiori weights.

Fig. 282: Kaziun weight with gold "K" signature.

Fig. 283: Kaziun rose cane.

Fig. 284: Kaziun stardust cane.

Fig. 285: **PAUL YSART PAPERWEIGHTS.** *Top, No. 1,* Large weight containing three flowers surrounded by a garland of canes. *Second row, No. 2,* Concentric millefiori; *No. 3,* Star shaped millefiori design. *Center, No. 4,* Magnum weight with a butterfly within a wreath of millefiori canes. *Lower row, No. 5,* Panel weight; *No. 6,* Concentric millefiori. *Bottom, No. 7,* Flower bouquet tied with a ribbon.

Paul Ysart

Paul Ysart was born in Barcelona, Spain in 1904 to a family of glassworkers. The Ysarts migrated from Spain to Scotland by way of Lyons, Marseilles, and Paris. In Scotland he apprenticed at the Edinburgh and Leith Flint Glass Works in Scotland. In 1922 the Ysart brothers (Paul, Vincent, Augustine, and Antoine) joined the John Moncrieff Limited Glass Works of Perth, Scotland, a firm specializing in the production of laboratory glassware and apparatus. Three years later the Ysarts introduced the "Monart" line of colored vases, bowls, and lamps; manufactured in the years 1925 to 1957, Monart glass was widely exported to the United States.

During the years at Perth, Paul became interested in paperweight-making. As early as 1938 he had created quality weights which were finding their way into important collections: two examples of his work, weights featuring butterfly motifs, are illustrated in the first edition of Mrs. Bergstrom's 1940 classic *Old Glass Paperweights*.

After Antoine's death in an accident in 1946, Sebastian, Augustine and Vincent Ysart started a new firm named Ysart Brothers at the Shore, Perth; Paul, however, decided not to join and remained for a time at Moncrieff, where he created some of the finest paperweights made since mid-nineteenth century. The Ysart Brothers manufactured some millefiori weights, but these do not compare favorably with Paul's work.

In 1963 Paul Ysart went to work at Caithness Glass in Wick, Scotland, as personnel officer, but paperweight production, however, remained his first love. Between 1963 and 1970 he produced over twenty different types of paperweights, working on his own time behind locked doors and marketing his productions exclusively through Paul Jokelson of New York.

In 1971 Ysart went into business for himself as the Paul Ysart Glass Company in Wick, Scotland; he now produces only paperweights and other glass objects, in very limited numbers (Figs. 285, 286, 289).

Ysart millefiori paperweights run the gamut of spacing schemes and backgrounds: from random to patterned schemes of all sorts and from clear to colored or lace grounds. His flowers are of the clematis type with leaves and stems but usually no buds, and are placed on jasper, colored, latticinio, or pulled-cane grounds; bouquets are similarly constructed. Some subjects are recessed into, and flush with, the ground.

The most popular Ysart motif is the hovering butterfly, which is featured on a variety of grounds. Other representational motifs include a butterfly over a flower, a lacy or decorated snake, a parrot, a dragonfly, three ducks in a pond swimming around a flower, and some very fine single and double swimming fish (Fig. 290). (The fish motif was also done as a two-dimensional subject in an earlier weight.) Inkwells and doorknobs have also been produced.

Most Ysart paperweights are signed with a small "PY" cane either in the design or on the base (Figs. 287, 288).

Collectors are strongly advised to acquire one of these fine paperweights while they are still available.

Fig. 286: **PAUL YSART PAPERWEIGHTS.** *No. 1,* Striped flower on a radiating lace ground; *No. 2,* Inkwell with paperweight bottom and stopper.

Fig. 287: Ysart signature cane.

Fig. 288: Ysart paper label.

Fig. 289: Paul Ysart parrot.

Fig. 290: Paul Ysart double fish.

Harold J. Hacker

When Harold Hacker moved to the West Coast in 1942, he found to his surprise that many of his former colleagues in West Virginia's glass houses had also migrated to the L.A. area. Drawing on his previously acquired skills in the areas of gathering and blowing glass, Harold began work at the Technical Glass Company. From there he moved to the Douglas Aircraft machine shop where he worked just eight weeks before he was drafted into the 14th Armored Division, with which he spent two and a half years.

After returning from the war, Hacker established the glass concession at Knott's Berry Farm, a Los Angeles area amusement park. He built up a successful business making intricate glass figures produced by manipulating colored and clear glass rods over a torch. Mrs. Hacker and other assistants all helped in the production, but it was never easy to keep the shelves filled with animal replicas, coaches, carousels, and intricate glass ships rigged with cascading loops of clear glass.

In 1966 Hacker read about a paperweight being bought at auction for over $14,000. The article suggested that weight-making was a lost art and that no one could duplicate the antique weights. Hacker had made some off-hand paperweights even in his West Virginia days and now quite an experienced glassblower and lampworker, he set out to convince skeptics that the art was still alive. Setting up a small furnace and workshop in a garage behind his home, and occasionally employing associates, he began limited production. During the day, in the intervals between making his regular lampwork items, he crafted the objects to be enclosed in paperweights. Leaves, stems, flower petals, stamens, animal components, fruit, and other minute pieces may have puzzled the tourists. After months of this detailed labor, he devoted innumerable evenings to the final — and most frustrating — part of the paperweight-making process. He began encasing the set-ups in clear glass gathers. Hacker chose to use the classic method of encasing elements in weights taking his gathers from a pot of molten glass. It was hard to watch an intricately-worked motif dissolve into a blob during the gathering process, as occasionally happened. Hacker persisted, however, and is now recognized as a contributor to the Paperweight Renaissance. (Figs. 291, 292)

Fig. 291: **HAROLD HACKER PAPERWEIGHTS.** *Top, No. 1,* Salamander on a sandy ground. *Center, No. 2,* Red clematis flower head surrounded by six colored flowers on leaves. *Bottom row, No. 3,* Central orange flower resting on a bed of leaves, with eight colored flowers surrounding the central bloom; *No. 4,* Large upright blue flower surrounded by six white flowers.

Weights issued under Harold Hacker's signature include an impressive array of motifs. Following is a partial list of subjects included in Hacker paperweights.

HACKER PAPERWEIGHT MOTIFS:

Bird on nest	Elephant	Parrot
Bouquets	Fish	Penguin
Deer	Floral motifs	Pig
Dog and rabbit	Frog on lily pad	Pine tree
under pine tree	Lizard	Sail boat
Dog	Mice	Snake
Duck	Octopus	Sulphide cameos

These paperweights are signed in one of three ways: "H.J.H.", "H.J. Hacker", or "Harold J. Hacker". Signatures, and sometimes dates, are written in script with a diamond-tipped pen (Fig. 293).

Fig. 293: Hacker signature.

Fig. 292: Swans by Harold Hacker.

145

John Choko and Pete Lewis

The era of paperweight making in Millville, New Jersey, was a 50-year-old memory by the time John Choko began experimenting with a torch in his workshop in late 1967. A corporate designer at the Wheaton Glass Works, Choko is a direct descendent of some of the Millville workmen who had created the renowned Millville rose. He owned a small paperweight collection which included a few of these early beauties. Admiring the roses by Barber and Larsen, as well as the modern versions made by Charles Kaziun and Francis Whittemore, he too was soon off in pursuit of the famous flower. His first efforts, marble-sized but containing all the glass his new torch could heat at one time, were disappointing.

Soon after, however, he was joined in the quest by an old grammar school friend and co-worker at the glass plant, Pete Lewis. Their first joint decisions concerned the manifest need for new equipment: a more elaborate torch was purchased and various apparatus was constructed; mutual encouragement and creative ideas were also exchanged.

The final results were beautiful pedestal rose weights. A variety of magnum-size salamanders, snakes, and flowers became Choko's specialty. Miniature flowers, including a Baccarat-style pansy set with a bud in clear glass interested Lewis. The weights are signed with a millefiori silhouette cane containing the initials "J.C." or "P.L."; date canes are also incorporated into some of their weights (Figs. 294, 295, 296).

Fig. 294: John Choko signature cane.

Fig. 295: Pete Lewis signature cane.

Fig. 296: **CHOKO AND LEWIS PAPER-WEIGHTS.** *Top, No. 1,* Black salamander with yellow stripes, resting on large green dahlia, by John Choko. *Left, No. 2,* Pete Lewis miniature pansy with bi-colored bud. *Right, No. 3,* Pete Lewis five-petaled white flower with pink "rose" center.

Robert Hansen

A professional lampworker from Bridgeport, Michigan, and a brother of Ronald (see below), Robert Hansen runs a small novelty shop where he produces glass animals, boats, etc. Weight-making is not his specialty, but he certainly has a talent for it if the few weights he has manufactured are any indication. Most notable of his creations is a lily-of-the-valley paperweight patterned after the famous Clichy example. His weights are signed with a full signature in script on the base.

Ronald Hansen

Years ago walking along the railroad tracks near his childhood home in Minnesota, Ronald Hansen espied two hobo craftsmen — possible immigrants from some Eastern European county — at work: using a charcoal fire and improvising bellows they were manufacturing glass ships out of soda bottles sawed in two. Such was Ronald Hansen's introduction to glass.

Pursuing a career as a glass blower he specialized in the manufacture of neon tubes, but he rarely got a chance to express his artistic tendencies until he turned to paperweight-making. Using only torches, he has tried many of the antique French subjects, gearing his efforts toward the construction of many different types of paperweights, rather than the perfection of a few types. Unfortunately, weights flawed in production were not consistently destroyed and some have found their way into the hand of dealers and collectors, casting a shadow over Hansen's reputation. His successul paperweights, however, are collectible and are yet another proof that the art of paperweight making is alive and well today.

A. F. Carpenter

One of a number of glassworkers originally from West Virginia, Carpenter's career has included highly specialized glass work at both Stanford University and, most recently, the California Institute of Technology in Pasadena, California. Additionally, Carpenter was for a period of approximately three years the creator of some paperweights issued from Harold Hacker's studio. After his association with Hacker ended, Carpenter set up his own shop and began to create salamander and snake weights. These vary in quality, but many are well done. They are signed on the base in script.

Carolyn M. and Hugh E. Smith

Carolyn and Hugh Smith have the distinction of being the only married couple working as a team to produce lampwork paperweights. Hugh Smith is a civil service employee.

Mr. Smith's interest in paperweights began in late 1960. Intrigued with the numerous design possibilities manifested in his collection, he began to consider planning and executing his own weights. He consequently spent much time studying glass and the artists who use it as their medium. An opportunity to attempt paperweight manufacture on a visit to the studio of a pot worker ended in disaster (for the paperweight). His determination to learn how to produce paperweights was strengthened by the experience.

With only crude tools and a very small burner, Hugh Smith spent many long hours at home studying lampworking techniques. His first breakthrough was the successful manufacture of a few button-sized weights. Deciding to go into paperweight manufacturing in a big way, he built his own workshop.

It was while assisting her husband in the new studio that Carolyn Smith first became interested in the art of paperweight manufacture, and particularly in possibilities for color combinations. After a while she set up her own bench and is now making a variety of floral designs (Fig. 301).

Smith paperweights are signed with a color-coded millefiori initial cane, either "HS" or "CS". The colors denote the year the weight was completed. An etched script signature is also found on the underside of most of their weights (Figs. 297, 298, 299, 300).

We can expect to see much good work from the Smiths in coming years, with continuing improvement in color and quality.

Fig. 297: Carolyn Smith signature cane.

Fig. 298: Carolyn Smith script signature.

Fig. 299: Hugh Smith signature cane.

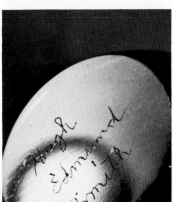

Fig. 300: Hugh Smith script signature.

Fig. 301: **CAROLYN AND HUGH SMITH.** *Top row, No. 1,* Poinsettia with bud on jasper ground, (H.S.); *No. 2,* Clematis on jasper ground, (H.S.). *Middle row, No. 3,* Purple Clematis on matching ground, (C.S.); *No. 4,* Fuchsia, (H.S.). *Bottom row, No. 5,* Unusual morning glory on a jasper ground, (H.S.); *No. 6,* Striped clematis flower head on five leaves, (C.S.).

Joseph S. Barker

A technical glassblower for many years, and now a plant manager in Newark, Delaware, Joseph Barker produced a number of flower and snake weights over a two-year period. These are signed with an initial cane or a script signature on the base. Because of illness and pressing vocational obligations, however, he has not produced any paperweights for some time.

Ray and Robert Banford

Perhaps the only father and son team making French style paperweights, Ray Banford and his son Bob are the most recent contributors to the paperweight renaissance. Influenced by other contemporary artists in Southern New Jersey and by the European factories, they have created a variety of interesting motifs. Single flowers, floral bouquets tied with a ribbon, bird-in-a-nest, trellis weights, and a dragonfly over various flowers are a joy to collectors. A most original design features a bumble bee hovering over a clematis type flower. Their work is extremely delicate and their paperweights are increasing in popularity.

Other Glass Artists

During the last five years, many new names have appeared on the growing list of paperweight-makers. Only time will tell which craftsmen should be considered to be important contributors to the Paperweight Renaissance.

Some dealers and collectors are confused by this recent proliferation of artistic endeavor. It is interesting to note that the best antique weights were made during a similarly active and competitive period, the Classical Period of roughly 1840 to 1870. Modern-day competition can only serve to increase technical proficiency and artistic achievement.

Chapter VI

New Directions in Paperweights

Recently, paperweights have become an important item at glass factories and studios developing totally new techniques and concepts in glass design. Some modern artists are working in a vein first uncovered by Tiffany in the mid-twentieth century. Still others ascribe to varied sources of influence. In any event, no serious collector should overlook the beautiful paperweights being crafted in contemporary idioms.

Dominick Labino (Figs. 302, 303, 304, 305)

A native of Pennsylvania, Dominick Labino studied at the Carnegie Institute of Technology and the School of Design of the Toledo, Ohio, Museum of Art. By the time of his retirement in 1965, he had risen to the position of Vice President and Director of Research and Development at Johns-Manville Fiber Glass, Inc.; he has taken fifty-six patents on glass compositions and processes.

Three years before his retirement his role in a three-week seminar on glass at the Toledo Museum directed his attention to the art of glassblowing. He had already planned to build a workshop to enable the continuance of his research into glass production. The concept was now expanded to include the production and control of color and form in art glass. One part of the self-educational process he embarked upon after becoming interested in glass art was original research into ancient glassmaking techniques which resulted in journal articles (e.g., "The Egyptian Sand-Core Technique: A New Interpretation," *Journal of Glass Studies,* Corning, New York) and *Visual Art in Glass,* a book-length history of the art.

As a true craftsman in the Old World tradition, Labino has designed and constructed his own tools, melting furnaces, and annealing ovens, as well as a number of devices for the testing and manipulation of various types of glass. One piece of equipment in his studio measures internal stress through a breakdown of light spectra, another creates minutely-diametered glass fiber. He has developed formulae for glass colors that are controllable and yield highly consistent and predictable results.

Artistically, Labino is as eclectic and ingenious as he is technical. His glass work ranges from floral paperweights to abstract sculptures. It also include such unique items as a seven-coated millefiori rod and a series of objects featuring external decorations. The control he exercises over the chemical composition of his "metal" allows him to create special effects. Many of his free-form vases, sculptures, and paperweights look totally different under direct, reflected, artificial, or natural light. Labino has produced prizewinning, nationally-acclaimed art pieces and can certainly be associated with the Paperweight Renaissance both as a progenitor and as a leading participant.

Labino paperweights are made from both clear and colored glasses. Their shape is conventional, but the internal motifs are created using colored and/or iridescent glass or air entrapments to form abstract designs. No crimps or molds are used. A particularly pleasing paperweight contains a pattern of entrapped air bubbles beneath a thin gold veil. Labino's weights are all signed and dated in script on the base. Designs include:

Air enclosures, sometimes with a gold veil, in clear or green glass;
Coiled snakes on iridescent grounds in green or clear glass;
"Cow-jumped-over-the-moon" motif, an abstraction on an iridescent cushion;
Free-form flowers floating on iridescent gold veils encased in green glass;
Upright tulips — a patented design featuring six or more petals crafted three-at-a-time — surrounded by gold veils;
Abstractions in clear or colored glass surroundings.

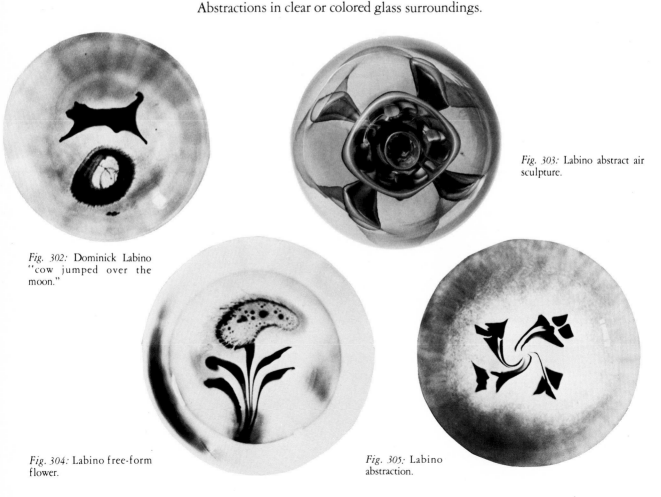

Fig. 303: Labino abstract air sculpture.

Fig. 302: Dominick Labino "cow jumped over the moon."

Fig. 304: Labino free-form flower.

Fig. 305: Labino abstraction.

Lundberg Studios

In 1967 while majoring in art at San Jose State University, James Lundberg attended one of the first college classes in glassblowing ever offered on the west coast. He had happened upon the beginnings of a renaissance in glassblowing. The "small studio" of the glass maker was just beginning.

Lundberg, classically trained in ceramics, found glass more suited to his temperament and the need for instant gratification in his work. "Glass isn't a waiting process like ceramics. There is much preparation in glassblowing, but once you begin to work, you work quickly."

Right under the incoming flight pattern to the San Jose airport he put together a "second-hand" studio, constructed mainly of junkyard finds. "I knew what a studio required. I had worked my way through college as a technician. I learned how to build my own equipment." New pieces and new designs sometimes required new tools, so he made his own — wooden blocks, torches, implements for grinding and polishing.

A graduate study tour in Europe took him to Germany, Italy, England, France and Spain where he continued his studies in glass. Upon returning to California, he met this author who saw his work and suggested he apply the same techniques to paperweights that he did to iridescent vases. By mutual agreement it was decided that L. H. Selman Ltd. would purchase all of his paperweights, thereby providing Lundberg with the economic security and time needed to develop new designs and equipment.

October, 1973, the studio moved to a small town just south of San Francisco to occupy the building that was once a bakery. The building, equipped with big gas pipes and high-powered ventilating equipment, with thousands of feet of floor space, seemed made to order for a glass artist.

Once in the new location, it was decided the glassworks would be run under the name of Lundberg Studios and structured in the studio tradition, with James Lundberg as master glassblower; Mark Cantor, first apprentice; and Steven Lundberg, second apprentice. The shop is run as a profit sharing co-operative. Others involved in various aspects of the operation are David Salazar and graphics illustrator Elizabeth Esteves, who is employed as a design consultant.

James Lundberg looks upon paperweights as a unique challenge. He is constantly experimenting and improving both iridescence and surface decoration techniques. His equipment too, is being updated, such as the recently installed computerized annealing oven. Lundberg and his team, however, find the greatest challenge in creating designs suitable to the surface of a sphere (Figs. 306, 307, 308).

Earlier this year they developed a Comet Kohoutek paperweight. The stylized design is not without its authenticity. Lundberg went so far as to contact noted astronomer William G. Mathews at the University of California at Santa Cruz. Dr. Mathews drew

Fig. 306: Experimental designs by Lundberg Studios.

Fig. 307: Lundberg Studios designs.

Fig. 308: Lundberg Studio designs.

up star charts so that the millefiori stars could be placed in somewhat realistic relationship to the comet in the overall design. When the comet, predicted as spectacular, fizzled, Lundberg lost interest. The experimental weight, pictured in Fig. 306 did though, bring about the use of an iridescent millefiori star cane.

Other experimental designs that have evolved along the way are also pictured in Fig. 306.

Designs produced at the Lundberg Studios, at the present time, are pictured in Fig. 308

The first of a series of limited edition paperweights issued by the Lundberg Studios is pictured in Fig. 307. The "Tropical Fish" motif was limited to 250 pieces. Mark Cantor and Elizabeth Esteves collaborated on the design. Cantor produced the edition.

Lundberg sees the avalanche of interest in his Art Nouveau inspired paperweights as "overwhelming." But his initial success has made him work all the harder. One of the projects in the future is adapting some of the classical French motifs to his iridescent colors.

Lundberg weights are in the Bergstrom Museum, The Chicago Art Institute, the Corning Museum and the Francis Fowler Museum.

Charles Lotton (Fig. 309)

An interest in iridescent glass led Charles Lotton to build a workshop, providing him with the space to experiment with glass and eventually produce paperweights and vases in the Art Nouveau style.

A beauty shop operator by profession, Lotton works in a small town near Chicago, Illinois. His business and family obligations do not allow him a great deal of time for glass. However, in just a few years he has developed the techniques necessary to produce a variety of pieces, some with iridized surfaces. Rather handsome King Tut patterned weights have been produced. However, his weights have yet to go beyond a few basic designs, although his vases show considerable artistry.

Many of the paperweights are not finished on the bottom and show a rough pontil scar near the script signature.

Fig. 309: "King Tut" design by Charles Lotton.

Fig. 310: Paperweight collection displayed in the home.

Chapter VII
Collecting Paperweights

Perhaps the primary motive for the paperweight collector is the satisfaction to be gained from the beauty of these glass objets d'art. Countless hours of pleasure may be derived from close examination of one Baccarat close packed millefiori weight. And the enjoyment that comes from possessing these bibelots is, of course, augmented by the challenge of the hunt. Good antique, and many modern, weights are not readily available. Much of the fun of collecting, therefore, is the discovery of a specific piece needed for a collection.

In addition to these subtle pleasures, there is the excellent investment potential of both antique and contemporary paperweights. The growth of their financial value has approached that of other elite collectibles such as fine paintings. A parallel may be drawn between good antique paperweights and old masters. A slow but steady growth in value is almost guaranteed. Contemporary paperweights on the other hand, are more like the work of an avante garde artist. Many editions from a modern factory will increase greatly in value immediately after issue, but appreciate less rapidly as demand levels off. A stabilizing influence in paperweight collecting is the fact that this hobby is recognized internationally, particularly in England, France and the United States. Collecting paperweights for investment alone is possible, but requires a thorough knowledge of the market and, ideally, a close alliance with a reputable dealer.

A most agreeable factor for potential collectors is the relatively small size of these beautiful glass bibelots. They take up very little space; can be displayed dramatically (Fig. 310); require no critical temperature control or upkeep; and are easily stored for protection from damage and theft.

However, for the serious collector, the real lure of paperweights is the intellectual challenge of finding, identifying and categorizing these treasures, and the aesthetic delight offered by an expertly crafted motif preserved forever in glass.

WHAT MAKES A PAPERWEIGHT VALUABLE?

Factors influencing the value of a paperweight are *design, workmanship, condition* and *rarity.*

Design, like beauty, is in the eye of the beholder. Good colors and pleasing arrangements of canes, flowers or other motifs are extremely important. Acquiring a first-rate paperweight collection, therefore, rests heavily on the collector's, or his dealer's, ability to evaluate good design.

Workmanship, on the other hand, may be judged objectively. Poor or faulty workmanship shows up in a weight as an imperfection. The collector whose prime consideration is investment should attempt to acquire only first quality examples. Familiarity with the following list of flaws will enable the collector to tell good paperweights from mediocre examples. *Few weights are flawless.* However, major versus minor defects will obviously affect the values of similar examples.

Checklist of common imperfections found in paperweight motifs:

Design not well centered.
Design too close to top of dome or sides.
Millefiori canes broken.
Millefiori canes unevenly spaced.
Millefiori canes missing or too crowded in garland motifs.
Concentric circles of millefiori canes distorted.
Leaves, stems or flower petals separated or cracked.
Leaves, stems or flower petals misshapen.
Spiral torsade or air rings incomplete.
Color ground or latticinio cushion broken.

The glass surrounding the subject should be carefully scrutinized and viewed from all directions. Imperfections in the glass have a direct influence on the relative value of a paperweight. The most beautifully crafted subject can be marred by a poor or defective crystal housing.

Check list of common imperfections found in glass:

Dark or yellowish cast to the glass.

Striation or fine thread-like lines in the glass; these are most easily seen when viewing across the dome.

Bubbles; these may appear in the dome or design. Most designs have a few tiny bubbles trapped around them. Large noticeable bubbles in the dome or design are undesirable.

Extraneous matter or pieces of firebrick trapped in the glass.

Condition of the paperweight must often be taken into consideration when contemplating its purchase. Scratches, chips and bruises may appear on the surface of the glass as a result of rough handling and misuse. If enough glass is present in the dome, the weight may be saved by grinding and polishing. In this grinding process, an even layer of glass is removed from the entire weight. The thickness of this layer depends on the depth of the damage. If the bruise is excessively deep, the resulting polished weight will be out of proportion; that is, the enclosed motif will appear too large, thus adversely affecting the appearance of the weight. Minor damage may be easily removed. A collector must be able to judge the effect grinding will have on the overall appearance of the weight.

Proper grinding and polishing on a paperweight with sufficient surrounding glass does not devalue it, but there are only a few *qualified* polishers in the world with experience in paperweight restoration. It is wise to check with a dealer before having a damaged weight repaired.

Rarity usually parallels the degree of workmanship. However, an unusual color, date or flower in a more common design may affect its value and availability. Many factors must be considered when judging which weights are more desirable or valuable than others. As a rule, the more complicated a weight's production is, the more desirable it is thought to be. The following generalities may be applied when comparing similar motifs:

> The larger the weight the better — except for miniatures under 2″, which are now enjoying great popularity.
>
> Color, lace or latticinio grounds are generally preferred over clear settings.
>
> Side and top faceting and/or cutting on the base is often favored over an uncut weight.
>
> The presence of certain identifiable canes, such as silhouettes and Clichy roses is desirable.
>
> Signatures and/or dates are an uncommon bonus in antique weights, but are imperative in modern weights. (See section on dates.)
>
> In floral weights, desirability increases with the number of flowers.

Rarity is, fortunately, fairly constant. Collectors and experts generally agree on which type of weight is more desirable than another. Quality and condition vary widely, however. Because all weights have at least very minor imperfections, the collector must learn which of these are acceptable and which cannot be tolerated. Novice collectors are often overcautious, and tend to reject otherwise good weights. Quality weights, even those with a few technical weaknesses, are excellent aesthetic and monetary investments. Needless to say, the most important consideration is the overall appearance of the paperweight and the ultimate decision to purchase should be made with this in mind.

THE LARGE COLLECTIONS

Most antique paperweights today are probably in museums (or on their way there). At least 2,500 good antique paperweights are housed in the small number of museums listed on the following page; most of these are in the United States. The largest and most complete collection of paperweights and relevant literature is located at the Bergstrom Art Center in Neenah, Wisconsin, where over 700 antique and contemporary paperweights are tastefully displayed.

Museums For Paperweight Collectors

The Art Institute of Chicago, Chicago, Illinois
Bennington Museum, Bennington, Vermont
Bergstrom Art Center and Museum, Neenah, Wisconsin
Birmingham City Art Gallery and Museum, Birmingham, England
Brooklyn Museum, Brooklyn, New York
Corning Museum of Glass, Corning, New York
Chrysler Art Museum, Provincetown, Massachusetts
Conservatoire National des Arts et Metiers, Paris, France
Cristalleries de Saint Louis, Paris, France
M.H. de Young Museum, San Francisco, California
Edward L. Doheny Memorial Library, Camarillo, California
Flint Institute of Arts, Flint, Michigan
Glynn Vivian Art Gallery, Swansea, Wales
Henry Ford Museum, Dearborn, Michigan
Metropolitan Museum of Art, New York, New York
Minneapolis Institute of Fine Arts, Minneapolis, Minnesota
Musee des Arts Decoratifs, Louvre, Paris, France
Musee du Verre, Liege, Belgium
Newark Museum, Newark, New Jersey
New York Historical Society, New York City
Old Sturbridge Village, Sturbridge, Massachusetts
Passaic Historical Society, Park Ridge, New Jersey
Peterborough Museum, Peterborough, New Hampshire
St. Mary's Seminary, Perryville, Missouri
Sandwich Historical Society Museum, Sandwich, Massachusetts
Smithsonian Institution, Washington, D.C.
Toledo Museum of Art, Toledo, Ohio
Victoria and Albert Museum, London, England

WHAT KIND OF WEIGHTS SHOULD I COLLECT?

The question of what kind of weights to collect is asked by all new collectors. First of all, it is necessary to become familiar with antique weights, modern makers and factories. Before making any major purchases, it is advisable to obtain all available books and literature on the subject. An international association of paperweight collectors in New York, headed by Mr. Paul Jokelson, publishes an interesting and informative bulletin once a year. Information about the association may be obtained from any paperweight dealer.

After a bit of study, the novice collector may develop some impressions about attractive types or designs. The recommended plan for the beginner is to start with contemporary limited editions or artist-signed weights. Many collectors begin by obtaining representative examples of most makers, both modern and antique. They then fill in their collection by adding different types which particularly appeal to them. Some collectors prefer only modern weights, while others collect only antiques. Very specialized collections may consist of only a single factory or maker. There is an infinite variety of possibilities, and the content of a collection is best left to the imagination of the paperweight fancier.

PURCHASING PAPERWEIGHTS

It has been estimated that six or seven thousand French paperweights have survived. A more probable appraisal is that close to 10,000 weights are extant, of which six or seven thousand are of good quality. With a large number in museums and perhaps a greater number in private collections destined to go eventually to museums, the supply of antique weights available to the collector is quite limited. Fine modern weights are also limited, either by the individual artist's capacity or by factory quotas.

Although the rarest and finest weights (both antique and modern) command top prices, an enjoyable collection can still be formed at a very reasonable cost. Among antique weights, scrambled and simple millefiori are the least expensive. Some modern limited editions are also moderately priced. Chinese weights can also form the basis of an inexpensive collection.

The three primary sources of fine weights are private sales, auction sales and dealers.

Private sales: Needless to say, there are few individuals willing to part with antique paperweights. Occasionally, a person with no particular attachment to weights will dispose of some which have been acquired through an inheritance. Less frequently, a disenchanted or pecunious collector will sell his collection. These opportunities are rare, and on the whole the chances of finding the right person at the right time are quite slim.

As dealing with a private party often entails coping with inflated price expectations (or monetary needs) and the lack of any guarantees, the doctrine of *caveat emptor* should (does) prevail. This method of acquiring paperweights is impractical for the collector.

Auctions: The possibilities of finding antique paperweights at small local auctions are few; special paperweight auctions are, however, occasionally held at the major sales rooms in New York, London, and Paris. The amount of time, effort, and expense involved in attending these auctions is prohibitive for the average collector. Moreover, it is hardly wise to enter the intriguing but perilous world of the art auction without a thorough knowledge of the object you intend to buy. The interacting factors of artistic appeal, condition, and workmanship are only rarely to be detected by reading auction catalog descriptions. A thorough familiarity with the quaint customs surrounding such sales and with the "language" of the auctioneer are also very necessary.

Dealers: As is the case in assembling any worthwhile collection, the collector should become acquainted with a trustworthy, knowledgeable dealer. The dealer's function should be to advise his client and to help him acquire desired pieces. In the case of paperweights, only a specialist can really perform this function. It is for this reason that the large majority of collectors' paperweights are sold through a small number of paperweight dealers.

Because dealers specializing in paperweights are few in number and widely scattered, buying by mail has become increasingly popular, as the collector may receive the pieces "on approval." This method is highly recommended as a practical source of supply, provided the reputation and reliability of the dealer are ascertained.

Fig. 311: Paperweights suit even the eclectic collector.

Glossary of Identification Terms

AIR RING . . . an elongated air inclusion encircling a weight near the base, usually above and below a torsade.

ARROW CANE (or CROWSFOOT) . . . a millefiori section made from rods containing a three-pronged arrow motif.

AVENTURINE . . . glass with a sparkling appearance caused by the addition of metallic crystals to the melt.

BASAL RIM . . . the ring around the bottom of a concave base where the paperweight comes into contact with the supporting surface.

BASE . . . the bottom of a paperweight.

BASKET . . . (a) an outer row of millefiori canes, pulled together underneath the motif to form a staved enclosure for the decorative element(s); (b) a latticinio ground pulled down in the center (as in St. Louis and American fruit weights); (c) a latticinio ground with a "handle" of twisted filigree extending above the motif.

BOUQUET . . . a floral design comprised of more than one flower.

BOUQUET DE MARIAGE . . . a mushroom-motif in which the tuft of the mushroom is composed of white stardust canes.

CANDY . . . adjective commonly used to denote scrambled millefiori weights.

CAMEO INCRUSTATION . . . another term for any type of sulphide object.

CANE (or FLORET) . . . The small piece of a molded or bundled glass rod that has been pulled out so that an intricate pattern appears in cross-section. (Refer to Chapter I for more detailed description of the cane-making process.)

CARPET GROUND . . . an overall pattern of identical millefiori canes used as a backdrop for a pattern of other canes or a representational element.

CHEQUER WEIGHT . . . a paperweight in which the millefiori canes are separated by short lengths of latticinio twists in a checkerboard fashion.

CINQUEFOIL . . . a garland having five loops.

CIRCLETS . . . small circles of millefiori canes.

CLEAR GROUND . . . term used for a weight in which the motif rests on clear glass.

CLOSE CONCENTRIC MILLEFIORI . . . a common spacing scheme in millefiori weights: tightly packed concentric circles of canes around a central floret.

CLOSE MILLEFIORI . . . general name for any spacing scheme in millefiori weights which features a tightly packed random arrangement of millefiori canes.

CLOSE PACKED MILLEFIORI . . . same as close millefiori.

COLOR GROUND . . . term used when transparent or opaque colored glass has been used as the background for a paperweight motif.

COGWHEEL . . . millefiori cane which has been molded with a serrated edge. This type of cane edge is quite common on silhouette canes.

CONCENTRIC . . . general name for any spacing scheme in millefiori weights which features concentric circles of canes placed around a central cane or cluster of canes. Concentric weights are either "open" (circles spaced relatively far apart) or "close" (circles close together), or "spaced" (millefiori canes set equal distances apart in vaguely defined concentric circles).

CROWN . . . glass above the motif, also called the "dome."

CROWN WEIGHT . . . a type of paperweight in which alternately colored and lacy white twisted bands radiate from a central floret near the top of the dome, flow down the sides of the weight, and converge again near the base.

CROWSFOOT . . . See ARROW.

CRYSTALLO-CERAMIE . . . The patented name and process developed by Apsley Pellatt. See SULPHIDE.

CUSHION . . . ground on which the decorative element(s) of a paperweight rests. It is usually convex in appearance when viewed through the top or sides of the weight.

CUTTING . . . grinding the surface of a paperweight for ornament.

DIAMOND CUTTING . . . a many-faceted cutting pattern used to decorate the outside of a weight: four or five-sided small "windows" next to one another may cover an entire weight.

DOME . . . see CROWN.

DOORSTOP . . . a very large paperweight. These were manufactured primarily by English bottle-makers and mid-western American glass houses.

DOUBLE OVERLAY . . . See OVERLAY.

EDELWEISS CANE . . . a while millefiori cane of star shape surrounding a core of bundled yellow rods — resembling the Swiss national flower.

ENCASED OVERLAY . . . see OVERLAY.

END OF DAY . . . see SCRAMBLED.

FACET . . . the level or concave surface formed when the side or top of a paperweight is shaped with a flat or rounded grinding wheel.

FILIGREE . . . see LACE.

FLASH . . . a thin coating of transparent glass applied to the base of a paperweight, or over the entire weight in the case of certain overlays.

FLORET . . . see CANE.

FLOWER WEIGHT . . . a paperweight in which a single flower is the central motif.

FLUTING . . . term for a pattern of deep narrow grooves usually cut vertically on the outside of a paperweight.

FOOTED . . . descriptive term for a weight having its own pedestal which is flanged at the bottom.

GAMBA . . . Viola da Gamba. A Renaissance string instrument played by the author.

GARLAND . . . general name for any spacing scheme in millefiori weights which features one or more undulating chains of florets forming a pattern.

GAUZE . . . see LACE.

GRID CUTTING . . . term for set of shallow narrow grooves cut into the base of a paperweight to form a grid.

GOLDSTONE . . . a gold aventurine glass used primarily by Italian glassmakers.

GROUND . . . see CUSHION.

HAND COOLER . . . an egg-shaped paperweight, once a common accessory for ladies.

HOBNAIL . . . term for set of V-shaped grooves cut into base of paperweight at right angles to each other, forming a grid pattern.

HONEYCOMB CANE . . . a type of millefiori rod, the cross-section of which resembles the cell pattern of a honeycomb. This cane is a Baccarat speciality.

INTAGLIO . . . a decoration either pressed or cut into the base of a piece of glass.

JASPER GROUND . . . paperweight backdrop formed by a mixture of two colors of finely ground glass.

LACE (FILIGREE, GAUZE, MUSLIN or UPSET MUSLIN) . . . white or colored glass thread spiralled around a clear rod. Short segments are used to form a paperweight ground.

LAMPWORK . . . term for manipulation of glass by means of a gas burner or torch;

a process of creating representational paperweight subjects.

LATTICINIO . . . a swirl or spiral arrangement of many white or colored threads of glass used as a paperweight ground. Lace (see above) is a type of rod, while latticinio is a type of pattern.

MACEDOINE . . . adjective used to describe a paperweight containing primarily filigree twists.

MAGNUM . . . a paperweight with a diameter exceeding 3 inches.

MARBRIE or MARBLED . . . descriptive term for an unusual paperweight design consisting of colored bands emanating from a cane at the top of the weight and running along the sides to the bottom, often in a looping pattern. The decorative elements of a marbrie weight are close to the surface of the dome.

METAL . . . old-fashioned glassworkers' term for glass.

MILLEFIORI . . . from the Italian phrase for "a thousand flowers." Used to describe the composite glass cross-section used in most antique glass paperweights. (Refer to Chapter I for details on the manufacture of millefiori canes.)

MINIATURE . . . a paperweight with a diameter of less than 2 inches.

MOSS GROUND . . . a paperweight ground consisting of canes made up of green rods. If such canes are centered on an "edelweiss cane," the ground is referred to as a "prairie ground."

MOTIF . . . the design; the internal decoration of a paperweight.

MUSHROOM WEIGHT . . . a paperweight containing an upright mushroom-shaped tuft of millefiori canes.

MUSLIN . . . see LACE.

NOSEGAY . . . term for a paperweight motif consisting of a flat bouquet using millefiori canes as flowers, set on a spray of green leaves.

OVERLAY WEIGHT . . . a paperweight that has been coated with one ("single overlay"), two ("double overlay"), or three ("triple overlay") layers of glass and then had windows cut in it to allow visual access to the inner motif. "Flash overlays" are coated with translucent glass before cutting. "Encased overlays" are double overlays with an additional thick layer of clear glass added before cutting.

PAPERWEIGHT . . . for the purposes of this book, a glass sphere or plaque enclosing decorative elements such as millefiori canes, lampworked motifs of colored glass, sulphide portraits, or metallic motifs.

PANEL WEIGHT . . . a paperweight in which clusters of similar canes form alternating sections separated either by exposed sections of the weight's ground, filigree twists, canes or rods.

PASTRY MOLD CANE . . . a millefiori cane which flares ("skirts") out at its basal end; this type of cane is found particularly in Clichy weights.

PATTERNED MILLEFIORI . . . general term for any spacing scheme in millefiori weights which features ordered groupings of florets forming a design.

PEDESTAL WEIGHT . . . see FOOTED WEIGHT.

PIEDOUCHE . . . French term for footed weight.

PINCHBECK WEIGHT . . . not a "true" paperweight as defined above, because not entirely enclosed in glass. A metallic disk with a raised design is covered by a magnifying glass lens, all resting on a pewter or alabaster base.

PONTIL SCAR . . . the characteristic mark in the center of a weight's base, where the weight was separated from the rod that had supported it during production.

PRINTY . . . a circular concave cutting on the outside of a paperweight — a type of window or facet. Also sometimes "punty."

PROFILE . . . the shape of a paperweight as viewed from the side.

QUATREFOIL . . . a four-lobed design used as (1) the central element of a millefiori cane; (2) a faceting scheme for the exterior ornamentation of some paperweights; (3) a garland pattern.

RIBBON . . . a flat cane, sometimes twisted, used in crown weights, torsades, and chequer weights.

ROCK GROUND . . . a granular, uneven paperweight ground formed with unfused sand, mica flakes, and green glass. It is sometimes used alone and sometimes as a supporting backdrop for snakes or salamanders.

ROD . . . a cylindrical length of glass, most often containing a simple molded design of more than one color; the basic component of a millefiori cane.

SAND GROUND . . . see ROCK GROUND

SCATTERED MILLEFIORI . . . a somewhat irregular spaced concentric millefiori pattern.

SCRAMBLED MILLEFIORI . . . a millefiori paperweight design in which whole and broken canes, and sometimes white or colored "lace," are jumbled together to fill the weight.

SET-UP . . . used interchangeably with "motif" to denote the central element(s) in a representational weight.

SIGNATURE CANE . . . a millefiori cane bearing the name or initial(s) of the weight's factory of origin or the artist who created it.

SILHOUETTE CANE . . . a millefiori cane which in cross-section reveals the silhouette of an animal, flower, or human figure.

SINGLE OVERLAY . . . see OVERLAY.

SPACED CONCENTRIC MILLEFIORI . . . a common spacing scheme in millefiori weights: individual florets are spaced widely and equidistantly in separated circles.

SPIRAL . . . an opaque glass thread wound around a clear rod.

STAR CUT . . . a many-pointed star incised into the base of a weight for decoration.

STAR DUST GROUND . . . a ground made up of white star rods.

STAVE . . . a flattened glass tube, such as those used to form Clichy roses.

STRIAE (or STRIATIONS) . . . streaks of glass of different optical quality caught in the dome of a paperweight. Striae can give the glass a sugary or grainy appearance which is undersirable.

STRAWBERRY CUT (or STRAWBERRY-DIAMOND CUT) . . . term for a set of grid cuts made in a paperweight's base.

SULPHIDE (CRYSTALLO-CERAMIE or CAMEO INCRUSTATION) . . . a three-dimensional ceramic medallion or portrait plaque used as a decorative enclosure for paperweight or other glass object.

SWIRL WEIGHT . . . a paperweight design featuring opaque colored rods of two or three colors radiating in pinwheel fashion from a central millefiori floret. The design in a swirl weight has a flat appearance.

THUMBPRINT CUT . . . an oval, elongated concave window.

TORSADE . . . an opaque glass thread loosely wound around a filigree core, usually found near the base of a mushroom weight.

TREFOIL . . . a garland with three loops.

TUFT . . . see MUSHROOM WEIGHT.

UPRIGHT BOUQUET . . . a three-dimensional grouping of canes and stylized lamp-work flowers set on a bed of leaves.

WHORL ROD . . . a millefiori cane component with a spiral-like cross-section. Often this is used as the center of a cluster of star rods.

WINDOW . . . see FACET.

Bibliography of Paperweight Literature

Bedford, John. *Paperweights.* New York: Walker and Company, 1968.

Bergstrom, Evangeline H. *Old Glass Paperweights.* Chicago: The Lakeside Press, 1940; Crown Publishers, Inc. 1947.

Elville, E. M. *Paperweights and Other Glass Curiosities.* London: Country Life, Ltd., 1954.

Hollister, Paul, Jr. *The Encyclopedia of Glass Paperweights.* New York: Clarkson N. Potter, Inc., 1969.

_____. *Glass Paperweights of the New York Historical Society.* New York: Clarkson N. Potter, Inc., 1974.

Imbert, R., and Amic, Y., *Les Presse-Papiers Francais.* Paris: Art et Industrie, 1948.

Jarves, Deming. *Reminiscences of Glass-Making.* New York: Hurd and Houghton, 1865.

Jokelson, Paul. *Antique French Paperweights.* Privately Published, 1966.

_____. *One Hundred of the Most Important Paperweights.* Privately Published, 1966.

_____. *Sulphides.* New York: Thomas A. Nelson, 1968.

Manheim, Frank J. *A Garland of Weights.* New York: Farrar, Strauss and Giroux, 1968.

McCawley, Patricia K. *Antique Glass Paperweights from France.* London: Spink and Son, Ltd., 1968.

McKearin, George S. and Helen. *American Glass.* New York: Farrar, Strauss and Giroux, 1968.

Melvin, Jean Sutherland. *American Glass Paperweights and Their Makers.* New York: Thomas A. Nelson, 1967.

Pellatt, Apsley. *Curiosities of Glass Making.* London: 1849, reprint.

Pepper, Adeline. *The Glass Gaffers of New Jersey.* New York: Charles Scribner's Sons, 1971.

Selman, L. H. *Price Guide and Catalogue of Collectors' Paperweights.* Privately Printed, 1975. Yearly. Available from: L. H. Selman, Ltd., Paperweight Specialists, 407 Cliff St., Santa Cruz, CA 95060, USA.

Smith, Francis Edgar. *American Glass Paperweights.* Wollaston, Mass.: The Antique Press, 1939.

INDEX

Page numbers in *italics* indicate an illustration. Text references which include an illustration are also in *italics*.